The Seductive Art of Astrology

The Seductive Art of Astrology

Meet Your Dream Lover Through The Stars

CAROLE GOLDER

An Owl Book
Henry Holt and Company
New York

Copyright © 1988 by Carole Golder
First published in the United States in 1989 by
Henry Holt and Company, Inc., 115 West 18th Street,
New York, New York 10011.

Library of Congress Cataloging-in-Publication Data
Golder, Carole.
The seductive art of astrology : meet your dream lover through the
stars / Carole Golder.—1st American ed.
p.   cm.
"An Owl book."
ISBN 0-8050-1025-4 (pbk.)
1. Astrology.   2. Love—Miscellanea.   I. Title.
BF1729.L6G63   1989
133.5′864677—dc19   88-38187
                                                                    CIP

Henry Holt books are available at special discounts
for bulk purchases for sales promotions, premiums,
fund-raising, or educational use. Special editions
or book excerpts can also be created to specification.

For details contact:

Special Sales Director
Henry Holt and Company, Inc.
115 West 18th Street
New York, New York 10011

First American Edition

Designed and illustrated by Paul Saunders
Printed in the United States of America
1   3   5   7   9   10   8   6   4   2

Contents

Acknowledgments

I'd like to dedicate this book to those dream lovers, past and present, who perhaps unknowingly inspired me to write it.

I would like to thank my publisher, Judy Piatkus, as it was during a lunch together that this book began its life, Gill Cormode, whose brilliant sense of criticism and analysis of course means that she has to be a Virgo, and Susan Fleming, whose Scorpio instinct was spot on!

Without the help of Jayne Cooper of Canon (UK) Ltd, it would have been a difficult task to write, as my typewriter packed up a week before I began the book.

I also want to thank Robin Esser, my editor at the *Sunday Express*, for telling me about Burgau, on the Algarve where I went to write; and William Robarts, Alice Sharland, Marie Toscano, Isabel Golder, Brigitte de Viet, Ann Zahl, Gerald Jackson, Louisa Martin, Martino Ottini, Bob Sherman, Dave Price, Don Maclean, Bryan Bantry, Andrea Challis, Wendy Walden, Judy Cornwell, Jennie Cox (with a special dedication to my god-daughter Gemma), I.K., Harry, Tony, Ursula, Jeanine, Ingrid, Hazel, Peter, Mark Hayles, Max Davidson, Jed Mattes, and the many other friends everywhere who encouraged me.

With a special thank you to Mark and Alastair for arranging the photograph, and to Allan who took it.

Meeting the Ideal Lover

I don't want this simply to be another love signs book, telling you which signs you relate to best, and leaving the rest to you. I want to show you that the perfect lover of your dreams *can* be yours – no longer pure fantasy – once you make use of the seductive art of astrology. And while I can't physically *find* that ideal lover for you, at least with the aid of this book I can aim you in the right direction by telling you who could be top of your list, and where you could find them.

In most astrology books you are advised which sign you relate to best. Here, however, I describe in detail how you can have a relationship with *any* sign, even if sometimes you might have to work a little harder to find your best methods of communication with your potential dream lover. You will learn how to identify him or her – by personality, clothes, looks – and then learn how to become irresistibly attractive with your own looks, behaviour and style. Soon you will discover that, even if you are supposed to be astrologically opposed, you can still keep your dream lover by your side. The seductive art of astrology will make that captivating task so much easier!

You will learn how to conjure up every seductive wile you've ever heard of, and maybe you will think up a few new ones along the way. The more you know about and understand your dream

7

lover from the first, the easier it will be to make him or her yours. True love isn't something dreamed up by Hollywood film moguls or record companies − it's there for everyone to experience. Romance will never die, thank heavens! It's lurking in all of us, from impulsive Aries to dreamy-eyed Pisces; it's simply shown in different ways. So be positive, patient and *prepared*.

And remember that dream lovers may not always appear to be the perfect partners at the outset. They sometimes have to grow on you and you on them. With a dream lover born under the sign of Aries things could happen very fast. But if Taurus takes a little longer, what's wrong with that, as long as you get there in the end? With the seductive art of astrology at your side, who cares if you're complete opposites, and your friends tell you it can't work? But sometimes, of course, it *doesn't* work: think of *Dynasty* star Joan Collins, once a *Sunday Times* 'quote of the week'. 'I've never met a man who could look after me,' she said after the break-up of her marriage to Peter Holm. But maybe she had forgotten that her star sign is Gemini. Does a true Gemini really *want* to be looked after? And the very things people criticize about one or other partner in a relationship could also be the very things that hold the relationship *together*. Perhaps Tatum O'Neal's Scorpio personality sometimes thrives on John McEnroe's typically Aquarian unpredictability! Maybe Aries Andrew Lloyd Webber is happy to encourage the rising Leo star Sarah Brightman. And I wonder who is the most jealous of Scorpios Yasmin and Simon Le Bon, or what Mrs Thatcher would feel like if husband Denis wasn't a Taurean who's happy to take second place!

Perfect relationships *can* be formed from unlikely combinations, even if they are sometimes slow at the start, and a perfect example are Mike and Jane, one of the happiest couples I know, now with three fantastic kids. But if anyone had said after their first date in March 1965 that they would − or *could* − end up together, they'd have had to be clairvoyant! It wasn't until September that Mike asked her out again, he then proposed at Christmas, and they were eventually married in the following July. Astrologically, I can see all the reasons why he waited, for he is a Cancerian, and had to be *sure* before he proposed; Jane is a Libran, and Librans always seem to possess a unique ability to wait for what is worth waiting for. (I'm sure it would have been very different if she had been Aries or Leo!) They made all their decisions without knowing anything very much about astrology, and have now been married for 21 years. If it is possible to attain a perfect relationship *without* the seductive art of astrology, just think how much easier it could be if you are prepared to practise a few of that art's techniques. And that is just what you are about to learn.

First, have you ever thought that your ideal lover belonged to a specific element? The twelve signs of the Zodiac are divided up into four elements — Fire, Earth, Air and Water — which in turn affect the personalities of each star sign. The three fire signs, for example — Aries, Leo and Sagittarius — all tend to be very enthusiastic, active and enterprising. Thus I have devised a special questionnaire so that you can find out which of these four elements attracts you the most. Then your choice of a perfect partner will be narrowed down to three possible signs.

I will also tell you — sign by sign — the sorts of places these dream lovers of the Zodiac like to frequent, their likes and dislikes, the kind of work they may be doing, the sort of holidays they might choose. You'll learn how easy it can be to make a relationship with any one of them add extra sparkle to both of your lives.

Of course, *you* have to help the relationship along too, by learning more about your own star-sign image and how you can project it most enticingly. When you read the chapter on 'How Well Do You Know Yourself?', you will see just what I mean. There's always a way to *modify* certain characteristics in your personality too — that negative side of your sign — if by so doing you can attract a fascinating new dream lover into your life. You will discover that you don't have to give out a 'come hither' look every time you meet someone interesting — there are more subtle astrological seductive wiles than that. And there's no going over the top when you're trying to captivate a dream lover who is obviously shy. You don't want to scare them away, for that's missing the whole point of this book.

Astrological seduction will provide you with a multitude of

opportunities to show just how imaginative you can be. It will be a chance for you to discover more about yourself and your personality, and the personality of your dream lover too. And from your discoveries you can scheme (in the nicest possible way) just how to start this beautiful new relationship that is going to transform your life.

Start to believe in yourself a bit more, and in the idea that your dream lover *will* appear, and not just in your dreams. Begin to realize that you have the ability to attract what is right for you into your life. It may seem a bit like wishing on a star – but a little magic in one's life never hurt!

Always remember that seduction should be fun, and astrological seduction therefore adds a whole new dimension to the age-old game of love. It requires imagination, a sense of humour (especially the ability to laugh at yourself if the tables are turned against you), plus the determination to remain totally convinced that somewhere out there is the ideal lover for you.

Do your homework well on all the signs. Be honest about what you want. Ask a Gemini friend to give you a few tips on how to flirt if you're out of practice (for no one can do it better!) and start to play the astrological seduction game. The stakes may sometimes be high, but the rewards will be bountiful. You'll soon discover there's a whole lot more to life when you have the perfect relationship to keep you happy.

So get on and do something *now*. It's never too late to turn those dreams of love into reality. If you want a perfect dream lover in your life, it's time to make the seductive art of astrology work for you.

Just try it and see . . .

Who Are You Looking For?

If everyone was looking for the same dream lover, we'd really be in trouble! (It might be fantastic for a man in demand, although if he happened to be a shy, sensitive Piscean he would probably run a mile at the thought of hundreds of women marching towards him with passion in their hearts!) Most of us have different ideals, objectives and needs, and although, of course, there are bound to be times in life when we discover we have a rival for the object of our affections, that's not going to happen every day. So first of all you have to be honest with yourself, because if you're not, it's best to stop right here.

The seductive art of astrology will only help you win your dream lover if you play the game *right* and stick to the rules. It's no use realising deep down that you need someone who's basically stronger than you if you rush straight out and fall for someone weaker just because of that wonderful twinkle in their bright blue eyes. The seduction game is a skill — but it doesn't have to be like mastering the intricacies of chess. *Anyone* can learn to use the seductive art of astrology to achieve a happier romantic life. Of course, if you're an impatient Aries who expects results overnight, you could be disappointed at first; and if you're a Gemini who finds it hard to concentrate on all the things to be remembered each day, start making a list of priorities fast.

11

It's no use thinking about all the lovely romantic characteristics you want your dream lover to possess if you don't list the faults you're prepared to put up with. You can't have one without the other, and besides, it would be boring if you found a man or woman so perfect that you had nothing to complain about to all your friends. Just think how many times the conversation turns to the opposite sex, even when you don't intend it to!

I'm not disputing the fact that these days there are more and more ardent feminists, or men and women who are so committed to their careers that they have firmly decided to put sex second in their lives – or even further down their list of priorities. But deep down some of these men and women may still be secretly dreaming of that wonderful lover to come their way.

However, you have to think really carefully about all this, so it's no use taking a half-hearted approach to the way you analyse yourself and your inner needs. What do you *really* want from a dream lover?

Are you looking for an intellectual soulmate and don't care too much about an excess of passion? Are you a workaholic who needs someone who understands your need for success? Or is domesticated bliss your idea of heaven? At the same time you have to accept that some of the attributes you're looking for may go hand in hand with some you're not so happy about. That intellectual stimulation that you crave so much may come in a package that includes a lack of sensitivity to your moods. And someone who loves cosy evenings at home may sometimes become too much of a stick-in-the-mud just when you're feeling sociable. As you can appreciate, it's very difficult.

So, having decided you need a little help in picking your perfect partner, read through the following questionnaire. It's designed to help you find which *element* you're attracted to most, and that in turn will guide you towards the *signs* with which you could most closely relate. Your answers may overwhelmingly point towards *one* element, but I think there will probably be a fair number of other elements' characteristics that intrigue you as well. Sometimes you may find you want to tick more than one answer to a question, which could mean that you are attracted to two different elements. However, when you count up your score you will inevitably find that one element will predominate.

Get yourself a pen or pencil and, if you don't want to mark the book, use a piece of blank paper. Read the questions through, think carefully, and then tick off the answer to each question you find most relevant. The answers you give, when totalled, will determine which element, and therefore which personality characteristics, attract you most – and will therefore enable you to have a clearer idea of what, deep down, you desire from that perfect relationship.

— WHAT ELEMENT IS YOUR DREAM LOVER? —

Questionnaire for Women

The following questions will have an a, b, c or d answer. No cheating now! Be completely honest, because the answers you have ticked, when totalled, will determine whether your dream lover belongs to the element of Fire, Earth, Air or Water.

DO YOU WANT A DREAM LOVER WHO . . .

Q1. *Shows his interest in you by*

    a. giving you a come-hither look?
    b. playing it very cool, yet calculated?
    c. being a good listener?
    d. wistfully gazing into your eyes?

Q2. *First attracts you by*

    a. the sexy way he moves his body?
    b. his intellect more than his physique?
    c. his straightforwardness?
    d. seeming to have a spirit of adventure plus a good sense of humour?

Q3. *Tries to find out more about* you *by*

    a. asking you outright questions?
    b. almost reading your mind?
    c. finding out whether your interests match his?
    d. asking questions of a mutual friend?

Q4. *Takes the initial chemistry further by*

    a. obviously wanting to get closer but waiting for *you* to move first?
    b. using body language that means he thinks he's great in bed?
    c. showing all the signs of interest but behaving like a perfect gentleman?
    d. almost seeming to back further away?

Q5. *Is sexy in a way that*

    a. isn't immediately obvious?
    b. is intellectually irresistible?
    c. reminds you of a little boy lost?
    d. immediately raises your heartbeat?

Q6. *Has a technique in bed that*

    a. proves beyond doubt he's a kind and gentle lover?
    b. makes you feel you should have read the *Kama Sutra* first?
    c. is exciting from the word go?
    d. is poetry in motion?

Q7. *On the phone*

    a. wants a highly intimate conversation even if you're at work?
    b. never forgets to tell you how much he misses you?
    c. makes his point in the shortest possible time?
    d. wants to make sure you're really at home?

Q8. *When he first invites you out*

    a. wants to make it an adventure?
    b. expects you to cook *him* a meal?
    c. keeps you in a state of suspense until the very last minute?
    d. takes you to a romantic, candle-lit restaurant?

Q9. *Makes you feel passionate by*

    a. being very, very tactile?
    b. his stimulating conversation?
    c. the gentle way his hand brushes your cheek?
    d. suggesting you fly off to Paris for the weekend?

Q10. *Shows how important you are to him by*

    a. being jealous of your every move?
    b. loving to share little private jokes with you?
    c. never leaving your side all evening?
    d. making it an unstated assumption with every word and gesture?

Q11. *If you said you fancied a sexy film star would*

    a. laugh and get on with whatever he was doing?
    b. take it as a personal affront to his sexuality and sulk?
    c. lead you directly to the bedroom?
    d. give you a withering look and change the subject?

Q12. *Makes you think he'd be a good husband because*

    a. he gets on with his parents, and yours, so well?
    b. he seems to love children?
    c. you'd share an exciting life?
    d. he's obviously dependable?

Q13. *Has a personality that*

    a. is rarely moody?
    b. is romantic?

c. is all go, go, go?

d. is usually cool, calm and collected?

Q14. *If you have a disagreement*

a. never loses his temper?

b. has to win?

c. will find a fair solution?

d. would sulk but soon kiss and make up?

Q15. *Shows you he's boss by*

a. the way he tells you what to do?

b. his intellectual superiority?

c. being in charge of the finances?

d. making you emotionally dependent?

Q16. *When you're going out is*

a. on time with a bunch of flowers?

b. an unpredictable time-keeper?

c. sometimes unavoidably, but unintentionally, late?

d. on the doorstep before you're out of the bath?

Q17. *Shows his sense of humour by*

a. being able to laugh at himself?

b. the way he loves to make *you* laugh?

c. remembering all the funny tales he's ever heard?

d. inventing some wonderful jokes?

Q18. *Thinks you should dress*

a. in the latest fashion?

b. to make you look sexier?

c. as romantically as possible?

d. in classic styles?

Q19. *Wants to make you happy by*

a. buying you champagne to drink in the bath?

b. buying you your very own stocks and shares?

c. helping you with the mortgage when he can?

d. allowing you to remain as independent as you want?

Q20. *Only spends time with other women because*

a. he finds them easy to talk to?

b. he loves a mild flirtation?

c. he loves to make you jealous?

d. it pampers his male ego?

Questionnaire for Women: Answers

Q1.
a. Fire ——
b. Air ——
c. Earth ——
d. Water ——

Q2.
a. Water ——
b. Air ——
c. Earth ——
d. Fire ——

Q3.
a. Fire ——
b. Water ——
c. Air ——
d. Earth ——

Q4.
a. Air ——
b. Fire ——
c. Earth ——
d. Water ——

Q5.
a. Earth ——
b. Air ——
c. Water ——
d. Fire ——

Q6.
a. Air ——
b. Earth ——
c. Fire ——
d. Water ——

Q7.
a. Air ——
b. Fire ——
c. Earth ——
d. Water ——

Q8.
a. Fire ——
b. Earth ——
c. Air ——
d. Water ——

Q9.
a. Earth ——
b. Air ——
c. Water ——
d. Fire ——

Q10.
a. Fire ——
b. Air ——
c. Earth ——
d. Water ——

Q11.
a. Air ——
b. Fire ——
c. Water ——
d. Earth ——

Q12.
a. Air ——
b. Water ——
c. Fire ——
d. Earth ——

Q13.
a. Earth ——
b. Water ——
c. Fire ——
d. Air ——

Q14.
a. Earth ——
b. Fire ——
c. Air ——
d. Water ——

Q15.
a. Fire ——
b. Air ——
c. Earth ——
d. Water ——

Q16.
a. Water ——
b. Air ——
c. Earth ——
d. Fire ——

Q17.
a. Air ——
b. Water ——
c. Earth ——
d. Fire ——

Q18.
a. Fire ——
b. Air ——
c. Water ——
d. Earth ——

Q19.
a. Fire ——
b. Earth ——
c. Water ——
d. Air ——

Q20.
a. Water ——
b. Air ——
c. Fire ——
d. Earth ——

Add up the number of ticks to find out which element attracts you the most.

Fire ——
Earth ——
Air ——
Water ——

1st choice _____
2nd choice _____
3rd choice _____
4th choice! _____

Questionnaire for Men

The following questions will have an a, b, c or d answer. No cheating now! Be completely honest, because the answers you have ticked, when totalled, will determine whether your dream lover belongs to the element of Fire, Earth, Air or Water.

DO YOU WANT A DREAM LOVER WHO . . .

Q1. *Attracts you because she has*

    a. great sex appeal?
    b. a good sense of humour?
    c. a knowledge of current affairs?
    d. a forceful personality?

Q2. *Reminds you of*

    a. your mother when she was young?
    b. your first crush at school?
    c. the sex symbol of all time?
    d. the heroine in the most romantic movie you ever saw?

Q3. *Thinks that sex is*

    a. not something to be taken lightly?
    b. something that follows on from friendship?
    c. the best and quickest way to get to know each other?
    d. not the most important thing in a relationship?

Q4. *Makes it obvious that*

    a. she wants *you* to make the first move?
    b. she likes to be the dominant partner?
    c. she has no qualms about experimenting?
    d. she has saved herself for you?

Q5. *Is interested in you because*

    a. she shares your love of having a good time?
    b. she likes mental stimulation?

    c. she is looking for true romance?
    d. she feels secure with you?

Q6. *You fancy because*

    a. she's the centre of attention?
    b. she has that cool, aloof look about her?
    c. she's romantically appealing?
    d. she looks as though she'd make a good wife, some day?

Q7. *Makes you feel*

    a. like a little boy again?
    b. you're the only man in the world?
    c. even more keen, because she's so indifferent?
    d. that you can't wait to tear off her clothes?

Q8. *In bed*

    a. wants plenty of action?
    b. is romantic and tender?
    c. likes to relax and talk after making love?
    d. is interestingly unpredictable?

Q9. *Fulfils your every need because*

    a. she's a true romantic, like you?
    b. she's wonderfully dependable?
    c. she's easily aroused?
    d. she never bores you?

Q10. *You want your male friends to meet because*

    a. you're keen to make them jealous of your good fortune?
    b. you want to find out if she's a flirt?
    c. you're keen to get *her* views on *them*?
    d. you want *them* to see what true love is all about?

Q11. *Where outside interests are concerned*

    a. is more interested in you?
    b. likes to share yours?
    c. has lots of her own?
    d. is more interested in making a home for you?

Q12. *Is ideal for a relationship because*

    a. she wants to settle down?
    b. she wants to have fun and remain free?
    c. she fulfils all your romantic ideals?
    d. sexually she's the best partner you ever had?

Q13. *Belongs to a certain age group and*

    a. could be the more experienced older woman in your life?
    b. is tender, loving, incurably romantic, and probably much younger than you?
    c. is probably lying about her age, but what the hell?
    d. is the sexy Lolita type?

Q14. *If you have a fight*

    a. sends you a card to apologize?
    b. makes you sweat it out for days and leaves the answerphone on?
    c. thinks the best way to make up is in bed?
    d. bursts into floods of tears or sulks when she next sees you?

Q15. *At a party*

    a. will stay by your side as long as you want?
    b. goes off and does her own thing?
    c. likes to flirt but only if you're not looking?
    d. always keeps her eye on *you*?

Q16. *If you said you fancied a sexy film star would*

    a. tell you to go ahead and try your luck?

    b. throw a tantrum?

    c. immediately think you didn't love her any more and get out the tissues?

    d. show you her *own* sexual skills?

Q17. *You feel would make a good wife because*

    a. your parents would get on well with her?

    b. she's such a perfectionist?

    c. you're so sexually compatible?

    d. she fulfils all your romantic dreams?

Q18. *Has a personality that*

    a. never goes over the top?

    b. keeps you constantly surprised?

    c. is usually bright, sunny and full of fun?

    d. shows she has incredible sensitivity?

Q19. *Has taste in lingerie which*

    a. is totally provocative?

    b. doesn't look too extravagant?

    c. makes *you* feel very romantic?

    d. is obviously the height of fashion?

Q20. *Fulfils your expectations because*

    a. you know she'd never let you down?

    b. she's infinitely exciting?

    c. she's the fairy-tale princess you always dreamed of?

    d. sex holds no barriers for her?

Questionnaire for Men: Answers

Q1.
a. Fire —
b. Water —
c. Air —
d. Earth —

Q2.
a. Earth —
b. Air —
c. Fire —
d. Water —

Q3.
a. Water —
b. Earth —
c. Fire —
d. Air —

Q4.
a. Earth —
b. Fire —
c. Air —
d. Water —

Q5.
a. Fire —
b. Air —
c. Water —
d. Earth —

Q6.
a. Fire —
b. Air —
c. Water —
d. Earth —

Q7.
a. Earth —
b. Water —
c. Air —
d. Fire —

Q8.
a. Fire —
b. Water —
c. Earth —
d. Air —

Q9.
a. Water —
b. Earth —
c. Fire —
d. Air —

Q10.
a. Fire —
b. Air —
c. Earth —
d. Water —

Q11.
a. Water —
b. Fire —
c. Air —
d. Earth —

Q12.
a. Earth —
b. Air —
c. Water —
d. Fire —

Q13.
a. Earth —
b. Water —
c. Fire —
d. Air —

Q14.
a. Earth —
b. Air —
c. Fire —
d. Water —

Q15.
a. Earth —
b. Air —
c. Water —
d. Fire —

Q16.	**Q17.**	**Q18.**
a. Air ——	**a.** Air ——	**a.** Earth ——
b. Earth ——	**b.** Earth ——	**b.** Air ——
c. Water ——	**c.** Fire ——	**c.** Fire ——
d. Fire ——	**d.** Water ——	**d.** Water ——

Q19.	**Q20.**
a. Air ——	**a.** Earth ——
b. Earth ——	**b.** Fire ——
c. Water ——	**c.** Water ——
d. Fire ——	**d.** Air ——

Add up the number of ticks to find out which element attracts you the most.

Fire ——	1st choice	————
Earth ——	2nd choice	————
Air ——	3rd choice	————
Water ——	4th choice!	————

☆ *FIRE (Aries, Leo and Sagittarius)* ☆

If your dream lover is born under the element of Fire, be prepared to be swept off your feet by a fiery lover who definitely won't take no for an answer, and has usually never heard of patience!

The Fire signs are ardent, passionate, impulsive, enterprising, energetic, positive and optimistic. They are a great deal of fun, but they can also be very bossy, demanding and much too aggressive on bad days, and often think they know all the answers, picking an argument just for the sake of provoking you!

All three Fire signs have great qualities of leadership, especially Aries and Leo. Sagittarius, who is ruled by Jupiter, planet of good fortune, is often too busy travelling the world enjoying one

24

adventure after another to bother too much about climbing to the top.

Life with a Fire sign is hardly ever dull, but it can be hard to keep pace with these whirlwinds of energy, who sometimes need a lot of taming to bring them to heel. It's often when you're feeling absolutely exhausted and longing to relax that your Fire sign dream lover will have far more exciting plans in mind. You'll have to get your act together fast as a result!

In lots of ways these Fire signs are like children at heart, especially Aries who never seems to grow up! They're often like spoiled kids who want everything they see and don't care how they get it, but by the time they're adults they should have learned enough about life to know it doesn't always work that way. They have a genuine desire to make people happy, to make them smile and laugh, to shower them with little gifts (and big ones too if they're an extravagant Leo!) to show how much they care.

They are the initiators, people who won't sit still until they've achieved what they're after. But for a Fire sign dream lover, the thrill is often in the chase, and boredom can set in far too easily if there is no challenge. Much as they adore being in love (especially Aries and Leo), they can be incredibly selfish by trying to hang on to their freedom too.

However, life with a fiery dream lover will be something you'll never forget whether it lasts a week, a month or a lifetime . . .

☆ EARTH *(Taurus, Virgo and Capricorn)* ☆

With a dream lover born under the element of Earth, you will soon discover you've met someone with their feet planted very firmly on the ground, who certainly won't put up with any nonsense from you!

The Earth signs are patient, kind, virtuous and conventional, and can provide you with security, both emotional and financial. But Taurus can be horribly stubborn, Virgo's critical and analytical ways can sometimes make you scream, and Capricorn's somewhat pessimistic view of life often makes you want to shake them.

If you've met an Earth-bound dream lover, your affair could

take quite a while to get off the ground, and it's simply no use trying to hurry it along by being too pushy, for that could end up killing it stone dead. *Patience* is the name of the game (so if you're a Fire sign you'd better take a quick cramming course), as Earth signs prefer to be very, very sure rather than risk being sorry later. This doesn't mean Earth signs don't fall in love at first sight but you can bet your life that lots of them will be checking up on your past and your present to see if you're really a suitable match!

There's also quite a difference between these three Earth signs; Taurus is definitely the most sensual, while Virgo and Capricorn are far more reticent about making physical gestures of love. However, Virgoans with a touch of Fire in their charts can be pretty explosive lovers!

On the whole the Earth signs are like the element they're born under – they're solid, stable and always-there-when-you-need-them kind of folk. But just as there can be earthquakes, so there can be explosive scenes with your Earth dream lover, especially if they feel you're letting them down in any way. And it's not just Taurus who can dig in those heels and refuse to budge over one thing or another.

People born under this element tend to work incredibly hard. Taurus may sometimes be too inclined to take second place even when possessing the ability to be in command. Virgo is known as the 'sign of service', and Virgoans are always highly critical of their efforts . . . and other people's too. Capricorn has always been called the 'workaholic' of the Zodiac, determined to provide as much security as possible for the people closest to him or her.

I've often felt it unfair that some so-called astrology experts tend to dismiss the Earth signs as boring. Just because they put a great deal of effort into everything they do, and never give up half-way (like one or two other signs I can think of), it doesn't mean they have to lead dull lives . . . And I can think of a few dream lovers born under the element of Earth who were definitely far from dull!

☆ *AIR (Gemini, Libra and Aquarius)* ☆

Sometimes with a dream lover born under the element of Air you may not know exactly where you stand, which could make life more interesting. It certainly means you can't take anything for granted, so don't expect this dream lover to be at your beck and call from morning till night.

The Air signs are often bright, witty, talkative, imaginative and artistic. But if we start to break them down even further, your Gemini dream lover could be quite a flirt and often hard to pin down from one minute to the next; Libra's supposed sense of balance can be somewhat thrown off course by that famous indecisiveness; and with Aquarius you have met the most unpredictable sign of all, as it's not easy for Aquarians to demonstrate the love they may be feeling inside.

With an Air dream lover there is definitely a need for mental stimulation as well as the more physical kind! Anyone born under the element of Air tends to place a greater need on the intellectual capacities of their partner than the Fire, Earth or Water signs do. The Air signs think a great deal, evaluate their thoughts, and the Aquarians amongst them usually have ideas well ahead of their time.

The Air signs are definitely 'people who need people'; they enjoy being in good company, making new friends, having a busy social life, and, of course, communicating their thoughts and ideas – especially Gemini who will expect you to be able to discuss a hundred and one different topics at the drop of a hat.

Sometimes it may almost seem as though the Air signs find it difficult to totally commit themselves to one person – although in the case of Libra (the seventh sign of the Zodiac, and the one that relates to partnerships), this doesn't always follow. If you choose a dream lover who is an Air sign you may sometimes feel you're not getting as much feedback as you'd like; that there's sometimes a cool and detached approach to love. Somehow the Air signs find it much harder to express their emotions. Talking about them is one thing, but when it comes to the nitty-gritty they often seem almost shy about letting themselves go and being really physical.

Then there's hot air and cold air, of course. It's never the same all the time, and just because these Air signs may not smother you with passion it doesn't mean they care about you any the less. It's just they see things in a different way, which if you're an Air sign too will be much easier to understand. If not, don't be put off, any extra effort you make with these signs will be well worth while.

☆ *WATER (Cancer, Scorpio and Pisces)* ☆

A dream lover who is one of the Water signs will definitely ensure you're not short of romance in your life. The Water signs are warm, emotional, sensitive, intuitive, sympathetic, compassionate, highly imaginative ... and, in the case of Scorpio, highly sexy too!

We've all known Cancerians whose moods drive us mad; and Pisceans whose impracticality often means we're left to pick up a bill. The Water signs aren't always the most practical of folk, yet there are plenty of Cancerians and Scorpios who are excellent in business.

A dream lover born under the element of Water will lift you to the heights of emotional bliss, especially if you're the sentimental type yourself. But because these signs are so very sensitive there are sure to be moments when their happiness turns to sadness and that's when a negative aura seems to cloud their personalities, and nothing you can say or do seems to pull them out of it.

It's sometimes difficult for people born under this element to hang on to their inner strength, and they are more likely to need a lift than any of the other signs. But think about their element of Water ... which is always on the move. Like the tides, the Water signs have to have their highs and lows, so if you want a totally steady, dependable dream lover whose moods never seem to vary year in, year out, you'd better choose one from another element.

However, if you've been building your own little castles in the air for a long time, and wondered if you would ever meet someone who believed in romance as much as you, you cannot do better than find yourself a Cancer, Scorpio or Pisces. They have no doubt been feeling much the same as you, and could even be very disillusioned by the time you come along.

For while the Water signs aren't as impulsively headstrong as the Fire signs often are, when they fall in love they fall deeply and seriously. They want happiness ever after, someone to fulfil their dreams and never let them down. And, of course, if they're born under Scorpio they are also incredibly jealous of the life you have led before. let alone what you might get up to now!

It may not always be easy to blend your personality with a Water sign, especially if you're much more fiery yourself, but it's definitely worth a try, for the results can be more blissful than you could possibly imagine.

Just make sure you don't shatter their illusions though. If it's only a fleeting love affair you're after, these are not the signs for you. Even that sex symbol of the Zodiac Scorpio deep down wants more than that.

How Well do You Know Yourself?

From Aries to Pisces we all have our own good characteristics, but if we are truthful we have our bad points too, and nowhere is this more evident than when it comes down to the seductive art of love! Some people become totally obsessed with the object of their affections – whether those feelings are reciprocated or not. And then there is jealousy, which always tends to rear its ugly head at one time or another.

So why not try to learn even more about yourself? Discover how to project the best possible image in order to captivate your ultimate desire – the perfect dream lover – and discover some of the problems you're likely to encounter if you're not prepared to temper your 'negative' characteristics at all.

☆ ARIES ☆

With fiery Mars as your ruler (and don't forget that he *was* the God of war), you often rush headlong into a love affair as if you were going into battle, but the strategy should be different – and that's where your downfall lies!

Just because you love a challenge, your life doesn't have to be a constant battlefield, although if you try and explain that to the typical Aries they'll look at you in total amazement and say they don't know what you're talking about. It's true, I'm Aries myself.

You probably already know that your astrological symbol is the Ram, but it might be an idea to hide away those horns from time to time, especially if you've fallen for a dream lover who is obviously intimidated by your enthusiastic, but often far too strong, come-on approach! Sometimes you even come across as far too aggressive.

As an Aries you have boundless energy, and a wonderful zest for life that seems to overcome even the most traumatic defeats. You're a true survivor, and usually have a great sense of humour that attracts people easily to your side. Your positive approach to life is a definite advantage, but if you're a typically impulsive Aries you will probably remember you've fallen in love time and time again – and each time you thought it was Mr or Ms Right! What you need to learn about love is that it should grow and become deeper in order to be lasting, and your trouble is that you often become bored once that initial excitement has died down. Your inability to wait can be a bore too! It's about time you finally learned to curb your impatience – and remember that what is worth having is usually worth waiting for.

Because you're such a highly emotional and passionate sign, you need the challenge of an equally passionate and strong partner – someone who is never afraid to demonstrate feelings, and is a true romantic at heart. Prospective dream lovers are often attracted by your outer strength, but underneath you're often vulnerable, although you're determined not to show it.

You may feel you like yourself just as you are, and are not prepared to change one iota of your personality, but all I'm suggesting is that you tone it down just a little, to understand the value of patience, and perhaps sometimes to be a little less honest about yourself until you know your dream lover a little better. It will make you seem far more interesting.

— ARIES AND ARIES —

A dynamic combination this. Even if there are battles it will be wonderful making up! You both love the challenge of keeping the passion in a relationship well and truly alive.

— ARIES AND TAURUS —

All that Taurean sensuality sends shivers right down your spine. Taurus makes a wonderful friend and is as steady as a rock. If you need extra excitement, don't be impatient — Taurus can provide that too, all in good time!

— ARIES AND GEMINI —

Mental stimulation, a constant challenge *plus* passion. If Gemini sometimes flirts a little too much for your liking, it's up to you to be so fascinating that from now on the flirting is all with you!

— ARIES AND CANCER —

Domesticated bliss when the Moon isn't making Cancer moody, so if you feel your Aries flightiness is too much for the Cancer sensitivity, it's up to you to tone it down.

— ARIES AND LEO —

Sometimes it could be a fight to the finish over who will be boss. You should know all about Leo's pride and need to be in the lime-light, so it won't hurt you to take second place once in a while!

— ARIES AND VIRGO —

If you know that your Virgo is incredibly well organized and critical about some of your ways, it's up to you to turn over a new leaf, especially as Virgo's sexual skills can also equal your own.

— ARIES AND LIBRA —

An attraction of opposites that is one of the best. It's the perfect balancing act. There is plenty of romance and passion, but first you must use every wile in the book to convince your Libran dream lover that you're the ideal partner.

— ARIES AND SCORPIO —

The sex is sure to be great in this relationship, and if you're worried about that 'sting' in the Scorpion's tail, just ensure you don't give your Scorpion dream lover any reason to mistrust you!

— ARIES AND SAGITTARIUS —

Two free-thinking souls together but, as Sagittarius hates to be hemmed in even more than you, always try to keep it casual at the start, even if this dream lover *has* captured your heart.

— ARIES AND CAPRICORN —

It's up to you to convince the more staid and materialistic Capricorn that you're not simply a fun-loving extrovert who is always on the move. This is a great business partnership that can become a warm and loving relationship.

— ARIES AND AQUARIUS —

You're sure to be intrigued by that Aquarian unpredictability. If you feel you want a more demonstrative lover to satisfy your fiery desires you could try playing a little harder to get!

— ARIES AND PISCES —

True romance is fine, but remember you can't live in castles in the air all the time! This could be the perfect dream lover but both of you will have to develop a more practical side to your personalities if you want the love to last.

☆ *TAURUS* ☆

Maybe you don't realize how lucky you are. Venus, Goddess of love, is your very own planetary ruler, and has probably passed her feminine wiles on to you.

Slow, steady Taurus. Passion may be burning away inside but you're not like impulsive Aries, you prefer to take your time, to size things up, plan your strategy – and then move in. Sometimes, however, you're inclined to wait too long and someone else comes along before you.

Of course, if you're a typical Taurean you're probably completely set in your ways and won't relish being told you should change a few of them. That obstinate look comes into your eyes, your feet seem to be planted even more firmly on the ground, and you won't budge. That's fine, but then you've only got yourself to blame if your dream lover ends up in someone else's arms!

It's about time you stopped being quite so touchy, too. You're suposed to have a great sense of humour, but show me a Taurean who is able to laugh at themselves when things aren't going quite right in the romance stakes. You're sometimes much too heavy, and have such a strong will and determination that you can definitely be a bit off-putting on one of your bad days! So learn to lighten up a little, and don't plod around looking as if the sky's about to fall in.

Because you have a lot on your mind and there's a serious purpose in your life, it doesn't mean that you can't be light-hearted too.

No one is suggesting that you start to live a more promiscuous life. It's just that you do take every single thing so very seriously, and one of the things that often drives your dream lover mad is your unbelievable jealousy. It's often even more than your opposite sign of Scorpio would dare to show – and you get so bull-headed with it too!

Anyone who thought that only Cancerians were moody could be in for a little shock with you. You'll go along so far, but then it's best to keep out of your path – and everyone should avoid waving a red rag in front of you! But when you are determined to capture the dream lover of your choice, you are positively driven to achieve your goal. You're also bright, so find out everything you can about him or her and then make your move. Don't forget, waiting too long could mean disaster.

While no one likes a lover who brags about their sexual prowess, you know full well that your sensuality is a great turn-on when you're with your mate. Conservative in many other things, you're pretty bold in bed, and you're also wonderfully cuddly on those cold winter nights!

So forget about lurking in the background *hoping* you'll catch your dream lover's eye – get out in front and make sure you *do*. You won't regret it!

— TAURUS AND ARIES —

Your Mars-ruled lover will bring added excitement into your life, so make sure you're ready for it. Don't ever hang back and allow your dream lover's interest to wane!

— TAURUS AND TAURUS —

Two stubborn sensual sybarites together. This can be a perfect match, provided you're both prepared to be loyal, dependable and a little less obstinate.

— TAURUS AND GEMINI —

Talk, talk, talk – for once your Taurean patience may start to wear thin, as you need some action too. Let your Gemini dream lover see that a little more sensuality can produce some sensational results!

— TAURUS AND CANCER —

Two domesticated home-loving lovers together. You can cling to each other on those cold winter nights, but may have to use slightly more friendly persuasion if your Crab gets into one of those down moods.

— TAURUS AND LEO —

It's up to you to make sure that Leo's pride is never wounded, and that your own Taurean obstinacy doesn't create a barrier between you. So give in a little more lovingly if you ever have a fight!

—TAURUS AND VIRGO —

You two can definitely make beautiful music together, as Virgo is such a perfectionist and can easily fall under your spell. Show your expertise in a soothing and sensual body massage to ease away your Virgo's tensions after a hard-working day.

— TAURUS AND LIBRA —

Both are ruled by Venus, so passionate love can abound. Since Libra's charm has captured your heart, make sure you never bore your dream lover by being too stubborn with your demands.

— TAURUS AND SCORPIO —

A real attraction of opposites this, but since it could initially be based on pure physical attraction, you'll have to show you have something *more* to give.

— TAURUS AND SAGITTARIUS —

Even the most determined Taurean could find it hard to pin a Sagittarian down to a long-term contract. The clever way to do it is to let them feel free as the air, and to hide that jealous streak that lurks deep down inside you!

— TAURUS AND CAPRICORN —

You both secretly yearn for a secure dependable relationship that will last for ever more. If your Capricorn is not as sexually orientated as you, why not slowly but surely let this dream lover see just how blissful sex can be?

— TAURUS AND AQUARIUS —

You're steady and dependable, but Aquarius likes a more unpredictable lifestyle. Play a clever game here: make this dream lover realize he or she can't physically live without you, but can still feel inwardly free.

— TAURUS AND PISCES —

You're both romantic, but it's up to you to convince this dream lover that neither of you can live on dreams alone, and that a little more practicality will make your relationship even better.

☆ GEMINI ☆

Rush, rush, rush, talk, talk, talk ... Do you really have time for a dream lover in your life? And if so, will you be able to convince him or her that you truly care enough to make a relationship work in the best possible way?

The trouble with your sign is that since you believe that variety is the spice of life, and that sitting still is somehow bad for you, it's hard for you to concentrate on your priorities, let alone anything else.

If you want to project your image more it's not a question of learning to get on better with people, for you're already one of the best at that! You somehow have to be able to convince them that your reputation of being somewhat fickle and flirtatious has been gained unfairly, and that when you're prepared to give your heart it can be for keeps.

Never fool *yourself* though, for more than almost any other sign you know you need a vast amount of mental stimulation in a love affair to keep it going. Sexual compatibility is obviously important, but even the greatest sexual fulfilment will begin to pall if you have nothing to talk about afterwards.

Mercury, planet of communication, is your ruler, and the art of conversation will never die as long as there are lots of Geminis in the world! This is all very well, but anyone you become involved with will want a lot more than communication if the love affair is going to work.

You tend to get uptight if you feel someone is getting too close, so why not try to reveal a little more of yourself, figuratively speaking of course! Somehow you're much too inclined to keep things on a surface level, and it's not surprising if your dream lover sometimes thinks you're all words and no action.

Remember your reputation as a flirt has probably preceded you and that you may have a fair bit of convincing to do before you're accepted as someone who can be as loyal, loving and dependable as one of the less talkative signs!

And perhaps this is the right moment to tell you that you can be pretty exhausting with all that chat, and that it's time to make a firm resolution, even if it's not New Year. From now on you're going to try and be a better *listener*. Socially charismatic and blessed with unforgettable charm, you can be even happier if you learn to enjoy the pleasures of those quiet, intimate moments too!

— GEMINI AND ARIES —

It starts off as a big flirtation, a headlong collision — the one sign that could leave you short of words in bed — so make sure you don't let your attention wander and risk that Aries wrath!

— GEMINI AND TAURUS —

You definitely have a good listener here, and a sensual playmate too, so don't move on to talk to someone else before you've given the Taurus dream lover a chance!

— GEMINI AND GEMINI —

Possibly the most perfect soul mate you could find. You'll certainly have lots to talk about from morning to night, and you should even find that you agree about most things too. It's a good challenge for you to see who out-flirts who!

— GEMINI AND CANCER —

This home-loving sign will provide you with plenty of cosy nights around the fire. You might have to cut down some of your party-going activities if you want to keep that love alive.

— GEMINI AND LEO —

If you're prepared to flatter your Leo for ever more you'll have them hooked. You can even get away with a little flirting as long as they know it's them you really love and, at least, you'll never be lacking in conversation with the Lion of the Zodiac.

— GEMINI AND VIRGO —

Both are ruled by Mercury, but there the similarity often ends. Don't be put off by Virgo's worrying and fidgeting. If you persevere you could have something very good between you.

— GEMINI AND LIBRA —

Remember that Libra is the sign of partnership, and wants a relationship to be for keeps. Forget about sowing those wild oats – if you're prepared to settle down, you'll have all the romance you could possibly want with this sign.

— GEMINI AND SCORPIO —

A stimulating challenge in more ways than one. If you stop talking for long enough, you'll soon realize you've met the most passionate sign around. But flirting with anyone else will be taboo!

— GEMINI AND SAGITTARIUS —

You may be opposites but you definitely have at least one thing in common – you're frightened of a total commitment. But this relationship can be so much fun, it's worth taking extra care to make it last.

— GEMINI AND CAPRICORN —

The Mountain Goat is ambitious in more ways than one. It's a real challenge, for Capricorn wants a stable, settled life while you're known as a social butterfly. Tone down your image, for Capricorn is definitely worth hanging on to.

— GEMINI AND AQUARIUS —

Aquarius appeals not only to your mind, but can usually excite you in bed as well. Life can be full of fun and adventure, so it's up to you to make sure it stays that way and routine doesn't start to set in.

— GEMINI AND PISCES —

You care too much about what's going on today to simply dream romantically about the years to come. But why not persuade your Pisces dream lover to be a little more realistic without losing all that romantic bliss? It doesn't have to disappear.

☆ CANCER ☆

Naturally you feel that a little Moon madness is essential for everyone's life. You figure that since you're such a sensitive, romantic person, there isn't a dream lover in the world who cannot fail to be captivated by your charms.

But wait a minute, you've managed to omit the fact that you're always described as having moods, and as creeping into your Cancerian shell every time there is something or someone you don't want to face. You conveniently forget that sometimes you can be much too clinging and protective towards the people you love, and that when you're really in a bad mood you're a definite pain in the neck!

It's no use trying to get out of it by saying that because the Moon *is* your ruler, you have an excuse for those fluctuating moods, for we've heard it all before. Besides, not every

Cancerian indulges in bad moods, they can be controlled if you really wish it. So if you're out to captivate a dream lover who hates any form of negativity, you'd be wise to alter your pattern – fast.

The lovely thing about you is that when you fall in love you genuinely want to do everything possible to make your partner happy and comfortable. There's no denying the fact that you truly are the most domesticated sign of the Zodiac, and both male and female Crabs enjoy making a home for their mate.

You're a security-conscious sign as you like to save up for those rainy days you're convinced might one day arise, and, unless you have a Gemini Ascendant, you're not usually a flirt.

Incredibly sentimental, you hate to throw away love letters or little gifts that bring back memories of the past. But watch out if you get yourself involved with a really jealous dream lover – you could be letting yourself in for unnecessary problems.

Never lose your tender affectionate ways for they're a blessing in this hard-bitten world, but remember that your emotions will sometimes be bruised too. Sometimes your sensitivity can let you fall for the wrong person, probably believing that you and you alone can point out the error of their past ways and lead them along a much happier path.

Too many Cancerians try to be mother, father *and* lover, which can easily backfire leaving you dejected and alone.

You need someone who's your equal in bed and out! Someone who has a shoulder as strong as yours when things go wrong and who makes you laugh on the days you do feel down. In return you'll be the perfect dream lover too, and never want to roam.

— CANCER AND ARIES —

Aries may sweep you off your feet, so make sure you're ready for it! Although you like a relationship to build up slowly, and feel that all fiery passion is overpowering, it can be wonderfully stimulating too.

— CANCER AND TAURUS —

A comfortable warm relationship this, and you can cook each other wonderful meals with all sorts of wonderfully aphrodisiac ingredients to turn each other on even more!

— CANCER AND GEMINI —

That Gemini chat may sound wonderful and make you feel like a million dollars, so don't start to sulk just because your Gemini dream lover starts to flirt a little with an old friend.

— CANCER AND CANCER —

True domestic bliss at last! You're both incredibly tactile, and should have lots of cosy nights at home curled up in each other's arms, protecting each other from the outside world. Mark down when it's full Moon time though, so you know when you might both be in a mood!

— CANCER AND LEO —

While you yearn to be in love – Leo demands it – never let the vanity of the Lion get too much for you. Besides, you can be just as bossy as Leo when you feel this particular dream lover is going too far!

— CANCER AND VIRGO —

Just because you're so soft and sensitive you don't have to over-react to Virgo's somewhat uptight ways. And if you *are* in a bad mood, you have to admit you can't blame Virgo for criticizing you. Try to understand each other a little more.

— CANCER AND LIBRA —

There should be lots of romantic bliss with this pair. But you'll have to come up with the right tactics to persuade your indecisive Libra you're the perfect dream lover before too much time has gone by.

— CANCER AND SCORPIO —

Sexually there is sure to be plenty of passion here, but you'll need more give and take. You know that Scorpio is jealous and that you have a possessive streak, but try not to arouse that sting in Scorpio's tail.

— CANCER AND SAGITTARIUS —

Don't be put off by thinking that Sagittarius is too free and easy for someone who deep down wants their dream lover to be a dream husband or wife. Even a Sagittarian dream lover can be tamed by the right person, so why not let it be you?

— CANCER AND CAPRICORN —

These security-conscious opposites can get on really well just as long as you find the right way to break through to those Capricorn emotions, which are sometimes buried deep down below the surface.

— CANCER AND AQUARIUS —

While you may have decided early on that it's wiser to have a good friend than an unpredictable and unconventional lover, don't overlook the fact that love can change even someone as cool and detached as the Water Carrier.

— CANCER AND PISCES —

If life consisted solely of looking at sunsets together you couldn't wish for a better soul mate, but too many castles in the air would be too much. Try to convince your Pisces dream lover that you have enough practical ways for both of you – but make sure you can prove it too!

☆ *LEO* ☆

The power of love is never underestimated by you, but you sometimes hit trouble because you truly believe it is your *due*. You don't plead hopefully for tenderness and adoration, no, you simply demand it — and that can sometimes be your downfall, especially if you come up against another Leo looking for the same thing!

For someone who can also show one of the most lovable personalities around, that purring pussy-cat can all too soon become the raging lion, and then you're no fun at all to be with. You sometimes have an inability to let someone else be the leader and it gets very, very dull!

Of course you're a natural when it comes to leadership, and we all know you're full of charismatic charm, a wonderful host or hostess, an amazingly warm-hearted and generous friend and a passionate and ardent lover — but that's not enough.

You don't have to start going through life hiding from the limelight (as if you ever could!), but it wouldn't hurt to be just a little less flamboyant, and more concerned with giving compliments than receiving them yourself. You should also stop being so damned bossy — especially if you're a female Leo when you could easily put off the man you're trying to captivate.

And if you've fallen for a steady, serious, hard-working dream lover you'd better learn to tone down your extravagant ways. Of course you want to impress this new-found lover, but not at the cost of your bank balance, please. The chances are you'll want to spend even more on your wardrobe, buy the most expensive bottle of perfume or after-shave, and then, before you've got to know each other too well, you'll even start buying extravagant gifts. A Leo and cash are far too easily parted, something many a Leo's bank manager or accountant are well aware of!

Ruled by the Sun, its powerful rays have definitely influenced your sparkling personality — you can be great fun, a tireless pleasure-lover who certainly enjoys giving lots of pleasure too. It's about time you realized that your sunny personality is a gift in itself. It's always wonderful to be around someone born under your sign — but only until you start to give out the orders, and then you may find a lot of people have appointments they can't be late for. Leo, it's up to you. Be a leader by all means, but don't continually be averse to someone telling *you* what to do for a change – especially if they happen to be right!

— *LEO AND ARIES* —

You can be the leader of the pack in lots of ways, although it might surprise you when Aries makes the first move. Play it cool, it's good for you to take second place once in a while, and the two of you can make a very passionate pair!

— *LEO AND TAURUS* —

Physically, you may be very compatible, and if you're looking for a long-term relationship this could be fine. Try to make your Taurus dream lover develop more of a sense of humour about life too.

— *LEO AND GEMINI* —

Gemini is attracted by your powerful charisma and knows just how to pay you the compliments you love. So make sure you do the same in return, especially as this could be true romance.

— *LEO AND CANCER* —

While you love the limelight, Cancer wants quiet tête-à-tête evenings at home. You'll have to learn to compromise a little more and try not to show that you sometimes find too much sentimentality gets on your nerves!

— *LEO AND LEO* —

Don't waste precious time competing for attention! Two lions together make a dynamic duo, and you can have a wonderful time being lovable to each other. This is romance on a truly grand scale, so enjoy it.

— LEO AND VIRGO —

Remember that your fiery passion could frighten Virgo away. Never come on too strong at first, for you have to remember that Virgo is usually more insecure than you, and very, very critical.

— LEO AND LIBRA —

Definitely an appealing dream lover, and that Libran charm will captivate you right away. With luck the way you tackle life will help Libra to overcome that indecisiveness too.

— LEO AND SCORPIO —

If you can dominate this sex symbol of the Zodiac you're on to a good thing, but be prepared to have a jealous lover who certainly won't like it at all if you start to play around – even a gentle flirtation is too much for Scorpio.

— LEO AND SAGITTARIUS —

This should be the perfect blending of two Fire signs, but if you insist on dominating, and Sagittarius insists on being totally independent, you will have to use your sparkling personality to make yourself even more irresistible.

— LEO AND CAPRICORN —

You will enjoy the challenge of making this workaholic unwind, but you had better learn to curb your Leo extravagance if you've set your heart on this more materialistic and conventional sign.

— LEO AND AQUARIUS —

This free-thinking soul is your opposite sign in the Zodiac. At times you can definitely make wonderful music together, but remember to tone down your desire to dominate both in bed and out.

— *LEO AND PISCES* —

If you thrive on flattery — and what Leo doesn't — then Pisces is perfect for you. But both of you should learn to spend a little less, and to concentrate on the practical side of life as well as on your blissful romance!

☆ *VIRGO* ☆

The trouble with you is that you're often so self-critical that you sometimes feel you'll never be able to captivate the dream lover of your choice — and that's where you're so wrong. When it comes to love you can be just as seductive as anyone else, providing you stop worrying about what people are going to think if you let your hair down a bit.

Virgo is 'the sign of service' and it's about time you served *yourself* a little better! It's almost as if you came into the world worrying about what was going to happen next. You have a wonderfully witty, dry sense of humour when you choose to show it, but you sometimes come over as far too cool and collected. Even so, underneath that cool demeanour there can be a scorchingly passionate heart, and it just needs the right person to light that Virgo fire.

Of course you are incredibly choosy, and there shouldn't be anything wrong in that, but you do sometimes carry things too far. Try not to judge someone too hastily, for even though your power of analysis is highly attuned, it is still possible to make mistakes sometimes.

If you rebel against changing any facets of your personality you might find yourself missing a lot, especially if you frighten away the very man or woman you're desperately trying to attract. It's no use coming over as cold as ice simply because you're afraid to let someone know how you feel in case it's misinterpreted. If that other person has met you for the first time, how do you expect them to realize you're in one of your introspective moods?

You're possibly the most disciplined of all the Zodiac signs, but you can't necessarily expect to be totally disciplined when you're practising the seductive art of love. The old rules may have to be forgotten for a while if you're hoping to get what you want!

So from now on resolve to make self-criticism a thing of the past. Look at life with a more optimistic air and don't be quite so horrified the next time someone makes a pass at you, especially if you fancy them too!

— VIRGO AND ARIES —

Who but you could spot the vulnerability beneath that Aries ardour? In bed you can be fantastic together, provided you learn to be a little less critical of your partner's techniques.

— VIRGO AND TAURUS —

You won't have to try too hard if Taurus thinks you're the ideal soul mate, but you'll have to learn to relax a little more with all that Taurean sensuality.

— VIRGO AND GEMINI —

A meeting of the minds, but you'll have to learn not to over-react if your Gemini sometimes has a little harmless fun flirting with one of your friends.

— VIRGO AND CANCER —

Cancer makes you feel safe and secure. It's a comfortable relationship this one, and it's up to you to be as sweet and loving as possible so that your Crab doesn't have too many bad moods!

— VIRGO AND LEO —

You're initially dazzled by Leo's bright and sunny personality, so don't start looking for flaws the moment you begin a passionate affair. It's about time you stopped worrying quite so much and got on with enjoying life.

— VIRGO AND VIRGO —

You have so many ideas and ideals in common, and you're both more sensitive than you care to admit. You can make beautiful music together, so don't waste precious time criticizing each other's techniques!

— VIRGO AND LIBRA —

If you start analysing as to whether Libra is too self-indulgent for you, it's going to waste a lot of time that could be spent getting to know each other in a much more positive way.

— VIRGO AND SCORPIO —

Scorpio's sexual techniques could intimidate you at first – if you've never met a Scorpio before – but don't let that put you off, for this could be quite a thrilling affair.

— VIRGO AND SAGITTARIUS —

An optimistic Sagittarian could be just what you need in your life, so stop finding faults where there may be none. Never try to tie your Sagittarian down, for this dream lover needs to feel free mentally.

— VIRGO AND CAPRICORN —

Your goals in life could almost be the same. It might not always be grand passion, but by making your Capricorn dream lover feel contented and secure, you can work wonders.

— VIRGO AND AQUARIUS —

You should have lots to talk about. But if you insist on having a totally orderly existence and try to lay down the rules, your unpredictable Aquarian could run a mile, and show that Aquarian emotions aren't always quite so detached!

— *VIRGO AND PISCES* —

Opposite signs in more ways than one – the analytical critic versus the romantic dreamer – but don't start to criticize *too* much, for what's wrong with a little romance in your life?

☆ *LIBRA* ☆

Most Librans I know don't seem to have any difficulty in projecting their images in the best way possible to captivate the dream lover of their choice!

It seems almost unfair that as a Libran you seem to be blessed with an inordinate amount of charm, tact and diplomacy. And because you're invariably fairly indecisive about most things, you don't mind even when you have to play the waiting game, as it gives you a chance to decide if your choice was right!

However, it is that indecisiveness which can, when it is particularly prevalent in your personality, drive your dream lover wild even before you've become a couple! So perhaps you could try to be a little quicker in making up your mind about what you want out of life.

There is one other thing you should watch out for: in your desire to please you can sometimes attract the wrong people. You love company, and are sometimes too kind and generous to those who take advantage of it.

Socially, you don't need any lessons for you're adept at putting people at their ease and talking about anything from pure cocktail-party chat to the latest acquisition at the Tate or Metropolitan.

If you're a typical Libran you hate arguments, but make sure this doesn't lead you to give in too easily on something when you'd be far better sticking to your own opinion.

While you don't often require advice in the seductive art of astrology, there may be times when your usual Libran charms don't work as well as they should – which doesn't mean you have to sink into a decline. There may also be times when your Libran laziness comes to the fore, when you simply can't be bothered to get your act together and make the effort to go out and socialize. This is often the case at the end of a love affair.

Even so, with Venus, goddess of love, as the ruler of your sign, you should consider yourself blessed. Love invariably comes your way again and again!

If you're true to your sign you will never stop searching for the perfect soul mate, no matter what your age, so be positive about it and keep radiating that special Libran charm. If you use it properly, you will never fail to have the required effect on the dream lover you're keen to have by your side!

— LIBRA AND ARIES —

Sexually there's a great attraction between you and your opposite sign, but make sure you're not too lazy when confronted with all that Aries energy!

— LIBRA AND TAURUS —

Two Venus-ruled signs together – physically this should be great. If your Taurus is a slow starter make sure that you're the decisive one for once!

— LIBRA AND GEMINI —

You're both good at talking about how you feel, but you may need to give Gemini a little gentle encouragement if this dream lover is to fulfil all your physical needs too.

— LIBRA AND CANCER —

If it's emotional fulfilment you're after, then Cancer could be your sign, but you may have to cut back on some of your socializing and do a little more *à deux* entertaining to keep your Crab from getting moody!

— *LIBRA AND LEO* —

Make sure that indecision doesn't enter your mind if a Leo dream lover comes your way. You may sometimes resent pandering to those Leo whims, but a few extra seductive wiles will have the Lion purring for more!

— *LIBRA AND VIRGO* —

You should already know that Virgo is the analytical critic of the Zodiac, so it's up to you to make sure you're not too lazy or indecisive when it comes down to the game of love.

— *LIBRA AND LIBRA* —

A wonderfully relaxing relationship with a perfect soul mate is on the cards here. Good conversation, plenty of romance, a kind and sensitive lover – so don't spend too long making up your mind!

— *LIBRA AND SCORPIO* —

It might not be difficult to charm this dream lover, but first of all you'd better make up your mind if you really want all that sexual intensity. If you do, just remember never to make your Scorpion jealous!

— *LIBRA AND SAGITTARIUS* —

There will be lots of wonderful moments to remember with this relationship. But remember that the art of keeping this dream lover by your side is to let them feel they're still free.

— *LIBRA AND CAPRICORN* —

Just because you can't imagine ever getting old, isn't it nice to know that here you've met someone who really wants to look after you? If your Capricorn dream lover sometimes seems a little too staid and conventional, a little gentle relaxation is sure to help.

—— *LIBRA AND AQUARIUS* ——

This could be a strong attraction between two thinking people. If your Aquarian wants to keep things on a lighter level than you, try to come up with some imaginative ways to tilt the scales in your favour.

—— *LIBRA AND PISCES* ——

Since you need an equal partnership in every sense, it's up to you to let your romantic Pisces dream lover know from the start that you're not prepared to be a shoulder for them to lean on — not too often anyway!

☆ *SCORPIO* ☆

Giving advice to the sex symbol of the Zodiac on how to project your image more to captivate your dream lover might easily be taken as an insult. It's not wise to offend a Scorpio, who finds it very hard to forgive a slight, let alone forget it!

However, that last sentence sums up one of your faults. You really should learn to take things a little easier, to develop more of a sense of humour about life, and not to take every remark made against you quite so hard. You sometimes imagine a slight or criticism where there isn't one, and you're supposed to be so psychic too!

We all know you consider yourself as the greatest lover of all time — or a good percentage of Scorpios do — and maybe you do indeed have a technique that works, but a little less patting yourself on the back might not come amiss!

You tend to be incredibly jealous, which is also something you should try to tone down, especially if you know full well there is no reason for it. The trouble is that while you're inordinately curious about everyone else's private lives, you make a point of revealing as little as possible of yours which, you must admit, is not really fair!

If you don't like having continual references made to that 'sting in the Scorpion's tail', you'll have to make people realize that you can be one of the most loyal and loving signs around. Not *every* Scorpio has a roving eye and seeks sexual excitement around every corner!

Make the most of your magnetism. You have a charisma that is hard for anyone else to match – and one glance from your smouldering eyes can often have someone falling at your feet!

It's sometimes too easy for you to captivate a dream lover, and deep down you know you like a challenge. You also need someone who will stimulate your mind as well as your erogenous zones – so don't just go for someone you think will be great in bed until you've got to know them a little better.

Try not to be quite so power conscious. You're often motivated to choose a dream lover because of who they are and, without even knowing it, you could be using them to achieve a certain ambition.

If a love affair goes sour on you, try to resolve you won't be quite as sour and vindictive as you may have been in the past. It probably won't be easy but your efforts will be well worth while.

Stop living in the past. The future has lots to offer, and with your amazing intuition you always seem to sense when a passionate new affair is about to start. In that, you're luckier than lots of us!

— SCORPIO AND ARIES —

Aries has a childlike enthusiasm that delights you – but even if you do leave this sign standing when it comes to sheer unadulterated passion, make sure you never let this dream lover know that's what you think!

— SCORPIO AND TAURUS —

Your opposite sign in the Zodiac can be as sensual as you, although you may need to practise a few extra seductive wiles to break down the Bull's somewhat obstinate streak. Never let your love-making get boring!

— SCORPIO AND GEMINI —

Gemini's flirtatious ways may drive you wild, but they'll be a fantastic challenge for you too. Mentally, there is plenty of stimulation here, although you may have to work a little harder to convince your Gemini dream lover that you need action too!

— SCORPIO AND CANCER —

Cancer's protective and possessive ways may be refreshingly pleasant at first, but don't give this dream lover any reason to indulge in a bad mood because they think you're hiding something from them.

— SCORPIO AND LEO —

You both have your own personal magnetism and Leo's sunny personality will brighten up your sometimes sombre moods. You both want to be in love, and never forget that Leo needs constant proof of your adoration!

— SCORPIO AND VIRGO —

You'd better try to make it plain from the start that while you don't mind being criticized for some things, anyone who has something demoralizing to say about your prowess at making love is in for a hard time!

— SCORPIO AND LIBRA —

There's sure to be an attraction for both of you here. But try to take a little more time with your love-making, for Libra hates to be rushed and isn't always as passionate as you.

— SCORPIO AND SCORPIO —

Two Scorpios together could be the perfect match, both in the bedroom and elsewhere. But never let it become a power struggle between you two sex symbols of the Zodiac – vow not to be quite so intense!

— SCORPIO AND SAGITTARIUS —

You love the Archer's positive and easy-going approach to life, even if it does sometimes make you wildly jealous! It would also do you good to be a little more easy-going yourself, for if you're too possessive your Sagittarian dream lover could end up flying away!

— SCORPIO AND CAPRICORN —

Capricorn is searching for material comforts and security, and you're more interested in your sexual compatibility. You'll have to learn to live with the fact that this dream lover is a real workaholic, and it's no reflection on you if they're sometimes incredibly tired at night!

— SCORPIO AND AQUARIUS —

You enjoy finding out how and why things work the way they do, so if you can learn to fathom why Aquarians behave like Aquarians you could be on to a winner. But don't be *overly* passionate, for Aquarius is overwhelmed by too strong a display of emotions.

— SCORPIO AND PISCES —

You'll never become bored reading each other's minds, but unless you want to upset your sentimental Piscean all the time, you'll have to give up that underlying desire to play the field!

☆ *SAGITTARIUS* ☆

It might be more fitting for *you* to give the rest of us advice on how to project our images, for you are blessed with the ability to get on with most people. Your positive, outgoing personality ensures that you are never short of friends. There is one fault, though (yes, even Sagittarians have faults!), that can be very irritating, and that is your constant conviction that you are *always right*, which obviously sometimes you're not.

If you are searching for the perfect dream lover, it might be a good idea to tone down this 'know it all' side of your personality. You may not have even realized it existed — many Sagittarians don't — so why not ask a few of your closest friends if they agree with me, and you'll probably find I'm right.

If you get yourself involved with a sign who is possessive, you might also be asking for trouble, for deep down, while you might be yearning to find the perfect soul mate, you know that you need your freedom too. It's not that you want to play around with other people — although you sometimes enjoy a casual fling — but there's something in your character that makes you hate to feel tied down.

Sagittarius is known as the 'long-distance traveller' of the Zodiac, and indeed many of your sign like nothing better than to be able to pack their bags at a moment's notice and set off for pastures new! If you're out to captivate a dream lover who likes to stay put, therefore, you'll either have to compromise a little or shrug your shoulders with a philosophical smile and set your cap at someone whose personality blends in more with yours.

With Jupiter, planet of good luck, ruling your sign you can afford to be supremely confident that you won't be alone for long. And never ever lose your wonderful way of cheering the rest of us up with a smile, a lively remark or an optimistic observation on those gloomy days when nothing at all seems to go right — this is one of your greatest assets.

— *SAGITTARIUS AND ARIES* —

This is an almost perfect love match. Just make sure you're both totally honest with each other, and make sure that your Aries dream lover knows you hate to feel tied down too much.

— SAGITTARIUS AND TAURUS —

Sexually, you could be captivated by all that earthy passion, so try to accept the fact that Taurus is sure to be more security conscious than you, and may not be able to compete with your energy either.

— SAGITTARIUS AND GEMINI —

It is flirtatious, fun and exciting, and it's up to you to make sure that your seductive techniques keep your Gemini dream lover coming back for more!

— SAGITTARIUS AND CANCER —

Even if you are more of an outdoor person than your Cancer dream lover you can still find lots of interests in common. With your positive and optimistic approach to life you might even be able to banish those well-known Cancerian bad moods for good.

— SAGITTARIUS AND LEO —

You both adore the limelight and each other. As you're both Fire signs, your love-making will be fiery too. Never forget Leo adores being flattered and resolve not to be quite so tactless at the wrong moments!

— SAGITTARIUS AND VIRGO —

It does you good to be criticized from time to time, so you could find Virgo a stimulating dream lover. Deep down there could be a very strong attraction, but you'll have to prove you can curb some of your wanderlust tendencies.

— SAGITTARIUS AND LIBRA —

This should be wonderful, although if you love an energetic life and you've found a *really* lazy Libra, you'll both have to learn to compromise a little more.

— SAGITTARIUS AND SCORPIO —

Don't keep asking your Scorpio dream lover where he or she learned all those sexual techniques, for you might not like the reply. Always remember that while Scorpions might be incredibly possessive and jealous, they are also very secretive.

— SAGITTARIUS AND SAGITTARIUS —

It could be party time from morning until night, but you'll both have to make sure you get enough sleep. This relationship works best if you think of it as a delightful dalliance. If it lasts for ever, so much the better.

— SAGITTARIUS AND CAPRICORN —

Don't start to think you have to run a mile simply because Capricorn is often far more materialistic and conventional than you. Just think how secure you will feel inside, and how much fun you can have getting your Capricorn lover to see the more optimistic side of life.

— SAGITTARIUS AND AQUARIUS —

Adventures don't always turn out quite as you expected, as both of you want to feel free. Don't feel slighted if your Aquarian dream lover doesn't always show his or her feelings enough, Aquarians are often that way.

— SAGITTARIUS AND PISCES —

Pisces appeals to the romantic in you, although you may have to convince your Pisces dream lover that you're just as romantic, even if you don't express it in such a sentimental way.

☆ *CAPRICORN* ☆

If you truly want to learn how to project your image more, then you're first of all going to have to take some time off to digest all this.

You're one of the most diligent, hard-working, ambitious goal seekers around. You believe in the sanctity of marriage, in putting money away for your old age, taking care of everyone in the family and being a good upright member of your community. *But*, if you're now hoping to captivate a dream lover, you'll simply have to learn to cut yourself off from the more serious side of life from time to time — unless you've set your cap at another Capricorn, of course!

The trouble is that all your good points, and there are many of them, seem to have an almost off-putting effect when you're practising the seductive art of love! Even if you feel an instant attraction for someone, sometimes you're ashamed to let it show, and start to talk about the price of shares instead.

It honestly shouldn't do you any harm to let yourself go a bit occasionally, and you don't have to worry about being called promiscuous just because you flirt with someone you're attracted to. Just think what you're probably missing — for you can't live by work alone. You can enjoy a real tear-jerker film or book as much as the rest of us — admit it — and you need some real-life romance too.

Now you're probably getting worried that you're being advised to become impractical and more of a dreamer, but all I'm suggesting is that you add a few more assets to your existing ones. Try to develop more of a sense of humour about life, stop being the eternal pessimist, and take a more optimistic view of things. What you need are a few Sagittarian friends around to show you how!

Besides, since you're so concerned about what happens when

you get older, wouldn't it be nice to think you've found the perfect dream lover to share everything with you in your vintage years? The life of a Capricorn is supposed to get better and better after they've reached the age of thirty, and even if you've been disappointed in dream lovers you've had in the past, just practise that new-found optimism and you could find the perfect soul mate sooner than you think.

— CAPRICORN AND ARIES —

On the friendship level you can have a good relationship with the Mountain Goat, but if this is your dream lover you'll have to tone down some of your exuberant ways and not be quite such a child!

— CAPRICORN AND TAURUS —

You're both steady, determined, security-conscious folk, and that Taurean sensuality will be very seductive. It's up to you to make sure neither of you go on too much about all your hard work!

— CAPRICORN AND GEMINI —

Your first impression may be that Gemini is much too fickle for you. But think what a challenge it can be to tame the social butterfly of the Zodiac, and let this dream lover realize that you can be mentally stimulating too.

— CAPRICORN AND CANCER —

You have lots of things in common with your opposite sign of the Zodiac – a love of security and material possessions, for instance – but you'll need to demonstrate a little more sentimentality if you want to keep the Crab by your side.

— CAPRICORN AND LEO —

Don't immediately think that Leo is too egotistical for you, for if you genuinely respect what this dream lover is aspiring to, you will probably realize that a little flattery doesn't hurt anyone.

— CAPRICORN AND VIRGO —

Since neither of you necessarily desire an incredibly physical relationship, you could make a perfect couple. Just make sure you don't give your Virgo dream lover any reason to find fault with you.

— CAPRICORN AND LIBRA —

You're attracted by that Libran charm, but if you feel that Libra is too relaxed and easy going for you, it may be because you never relax enough yourself — so it may be time to start.

— CAPRICORN AND SCORPIO —

Definitely a powerful combination — you're fascinated and intrigued by Scorpio's reputation, so it's up to you to take time off from all your work to see if it's justified.

— CAPRICORN AND SAGITTARIUS —

The free and easy approach is just not in your make-up, but if Sagittarius seems too much of a gambler, perhaps it's because you're often too wrapped up in the material side of life. Develop more of a sense of humour to keep this dream lover by your side.

— CAPRICORN AND CAPRICORN —

Of course you are sure to admire your own sign, but make sure you're not both so wrapped up in your careers that romance doesn't get a look in. Even workaholics can have fun seducing each other!

— *CAPRICORN AND AQUARIUS* —

Wonderful for a fling (as if you'd contemplate such a thing!), but you'll have to try to be a little less conventional if you want to captivate an Aquarian with your charms.

— *CAPRICORN AND PISCES* —

You're often too earth bound to build castles in the air. All that Piscean romantic sensitivity should come as a pleasant relief so try to unwind a little more.

☆ *AQUARIUS* ☆

You probably don't even care about projecting your image in a more positive way — you like it just the way it is — and if other people sometimes accuse you of defying convention too much for comfort, you're even happier.

If you're still searching for the perfect dream lover to make your happiness complete, there are a few pointers that could help you achieve your ambition. For one thing, you often find it unbelievably difficult to show your feelings when it comes down to the nitty-gritty of romance. That cool, unemotional detachment might be fine if you've met someone who thrives on challenges — but if not, they could simply interpret your attitude as complete disinterest, which in turn could make them feel the same way.

Lateness is often one of your faults, although it can be because you've got more important things on your mind (or at least, they're more important to you). You dwell in the future and time to you is such a vast entity that your thoughts are often way ahead of the rest of us; which doesn't necessarily make it any easier for the dream lover who gets involved with *you*.

What is it within you that makes you want to be such a rebel? Is it perhaps that you're almost scared to commit yourself to anything or anyone because you know that someone as idealistic as you might all too easily end up disappointed? That's all very well, but if you're going to expect a commitment from your lover you'll simply have to knuckle under a little more yourself, and not be quite so caught up in your own little world.

You're so concerned with being unique that you sometimes overpower the dream lover you're trying to seduce by being too intellectual, too independent, or too concerned with the world as a whole to devote your attention to the person closest to you. Therefore, if you want not just to captivate but also to *keep* your new-found dream lover by your side, you might start pretending you're not quite as independent as you seem.

Remember that, since freedom is what life is all about to you, it's no use exhibiting any signs of jealousy if you've got yourself involved with someone who feels that way too!

It's sometimes been said that Aquarians make better friends than long-term lovers because of the way they like to run their lives; so if it's a permanent relationship you're after, you'd better improve on your tactics now.

— AQUARIUS AND ARIES —

You two can be wonderful friends, but remember that Aries is often lacking in patience and won't wait around while you're inwardly debating whether to have an affair or not.

— AQUARIUS AND TAURUS —

The Bull won't give up till you've given in, and if you'd only unleash some of your emotions you could be pleasantly surprised by just how rewarding this relationship can be.

— AQUARIUS AND GEMINI —

There's no lack of mental stimulation here. Just make sure you keep the romance alive for both of you by indulging in a little more bedtime play as well. Love can't survive on conversation alone!

— AQUARIUS AND CANCER —

All those kisses and cuddles should be positively blissful, so don't start worrying unnecessarily that so much cosy domesticity will cramp your style.

— AQUARIUS AND LEO —

It's true that opposites often attract each other, but you'd better make a resolution not to be embarrassed if your dream lover sometimes likes to show off in front of you.

— AQUARIUS AND VIRGO —

You're prepared to see the best in everyone, so even if this dream lover does sometimes have some pernickety ways, be pleased that at least he or she will do everything possible to satisfy you in bed.

— AQUARIUS AND LIBRA —

Since this blending of two Air signs is about as perfect as you could hope for, try not to be quite so cool and detached. Remember that Librans need romance in their lives!

— AQUARIUS AND SCORPIO —

If you were ever told off for playing with matches when you were young, someone might have warned you the selfsame way about Scorpio. Think of it as a challenge to tame this sexually fascinating lover!

— AQUARIUS AND SAGITTARIUS —

If you're looking for a casual easy-going involvement with no real strings attached, the sign of the Archer should prove perfect for you. If you want a long-term relationship, you'll have to let this dream lover retain that air of independence that is so much like your own!

— *AQUARIUS AND CAPRICORN* —

Once you've decided it's time to settle down for good, you'll have plenty of security here. But you'll have to convince your Capricorn that you're prepared to tone down some of your more unpredictable ways.

— *AQUARIUS AND AQUARIUS* —

Who else could truly understand what you're all about! There certainly won't be any monotony about this relationship, so just make sure you don't let this dream lover slip away by being too detached.

— *AQUARIUS AND PISCES* —

You want to see your ideals become reality, while the sign of the Fish is often content for them to stay as dreams. But it could be wonderful building those castles in the air together and *then* seeing them fulfilled.

☆ *PISCES* ☆

If you're content to live in a land of make-believe, convinced that one day a prince or princess will come your way without your having to do one little thing to guide them in your direction, it's about time you took off those rose-coloured spectacles of yours! It might happen that way in fairy tales, but life nowadays is vastly different from that of yesteryear. While it's wonderful to come across someone as refreshingly romantic as you, it wouldn't hurt to acquire a little more common sense.

If you stay as you are, the chances are the only kind of dream lover who'll stick by your side will be another Pisces who may well be as impractical as you. This may sound harsh, especially when you have such marvellous good points – you're sensitive, compassionate and tender – but you do tend to be swept off your feet by someone who is everything you *don't* need in your life.

Since you possess such a highly attuned sense of intuition, you really must learn to use it for your own protection. No more falling for hard-luck stories, no more being a shoulder to lean on (for someone probably infinitely stronger than you if the truth were only known).

If you want to captivate a dream lover who will be *good* for you, then you'll have to start by growing up a little. Not everyone wants a partner who continually needs reassurance, and periodically has to be a lent a few pounds or dollars because they've run out of cash yet again. Try to stand on your own two feet a little more often – you're so much stronger than you sometimes appear.

Be a little more outgoing too. Sometimes your shyness prevents you from getting to know someone who could be the ideal mate, simply because you're lurking in the background instead of being up there with the more outgoing signs.

You don't have to change *too much*, for it is refreshing to meet someone who still believes that true love does exist, but try to think a little harder about the future instead of dwelling in your own little world. Don't reflect on past disappointments in your love life for that will only make you introspective and negative too.

Believe in yourself more. Ten to one you're blessed with some sort of creative ability but you always tend to undervalue yourself far too much. With a new positive outlook, that long-awaited dream lover may not be a dream any more!

— PISCES AND ARIES —

Suddenly it's as if a whirlwind has entered your life. You've hardly time to pause for breath. Since you're both romantics at heart, it's also up to you to provide the challenge that will keep that Aries ardour alive.

— PISCES AND TAURUS —

This sign's dream castles are built on the ground, so if you want a steady, dependable, Taurean dream lover you'll have to brush up on a few more practical issues too.

— PISCES AND GEMINI —

You're swept off your feet by all that charm, but don't become too sentimental until you've got to know this dream lover a little better. It might be an idea to practise a little flirting too, since Gemini knows all about that!

— PISCES AND CANCER —

Could there ever be two more romantic people? But make sure your relationship doesn't ever become too wishy-washy – you have to excite each other too!

— PISCES AND LEO —

It's true that Leo adores being in love, so don't moan if you sometimes feel it's a more selfish kind of love than yours. If you remember that Leo can't help wanting to be the star of the show you'll be halfway there!

— PISCES AND VIRGO —

Your opposite sign in the Zodiac may sometimes irritate you with some of those typical Virgoan idiosyncracies, but a little Piscean tenderness will go a long way to convince this dream lover that you can be a perfect soul mate.

— PISCES AND LIBRA —

There can be such wonderful communication between you two – don't spoil it all by taking nearly as long as Libra to make up your mind on whether this dream lover is really right for you!

— PISCES AND SCORPIO —

Just because this sign is so blatantly sexual, you don't have to run away in fear. Learn to overcome your timidity and shyness, for you might be surprised by just how romantic this dream lover can be too.

— PISCES AND SAGITTARIUS —

You may sometimes wish you could be as outgoing and sociable as Sagittarius – who may in turn yearn to be as sentimental as you. With both of you learning more about each other a loving friendship can develop into a wonderful affair.

— PISCES AND CAPRICORN —

Just make sure your impractical ways don't send this practical sign straight into the arms of another Capricorn! If you want to catch the Mountain Goat you'd better forget about dreaming beautiful dreams all day long, and take a quick book-keeping course!

— PISCES AND AQUARIUS —

Since Aquarius isn't good at expressing emotions, you might think it would be hard for this dream lover to fulfil all your romantic expectations – but why not try to be a little more unpredictable in order to captivate this sign?

— PISCES AND PISCES —

True romance is all very well, but don't think you can get away with whispering sweet nothings in each others' ears for ever more. You'll both have to keep the other interested in more ways than that.

The Dream Lovers

The Aries Dream Lover

☆ The Aries Man ☆

Are you ready for a perpetual challenge in your life? If so, remember that Mars, the God of war, is the ruler of Aries, first of the Fire signs. An Aries man can be one of the most fascinating characters you have ever met — but you're sure to have lots of battles too.

Aries wants to be the hunter, the dashing lover who calls the tune. The best way to captivate him is to retain an air of mystery. This man must never feel completely secure about you, for once it's obvious that you could be there for keeps the Aries interest can quickly wane.

While he may bombard you with flowers, telephone calls and romantic dinners, it should never be you who initiates things. To capture and keep this man you must be prepared to play the waiting game: make sure you're often out when he calls (even if you're not), and don't always return his frantic messages on your answering machine. Aries wants the elusive: it stimulates his emotions and his fiery passion, making him want to see you even more.

The first day of Aries coincides with the first day of spring, and Ariens possess that wonderful enthusiasm and energy that seems to tie in with how we feel then — when suddenly the dull and dismal weather starts to lift, flowers begin to bloom and there's a different feeling in the air. If you are bowled over by this man's outgoing personality, by the way he treats you as if you were the first woman in the world, by the inner strength he radiates, watch out! You could be hooked faster than you think, and you have a lot to learn.

Every astrological sign rules a certain part of the body and it's not difficult to accept that Aries rules the head — always a striking physical feature with this sign. Think of movie stars like Spencer Tracy, Marlon Brando, Rod Steiger, and what about Warren Beatty, who might easily personify just about everyone's idea of the perfect dream lover? Think how magnetic their faces are. Even if you usually have a hard time guessing somebody's sign, it may become a *fait accompli* when you meet an Aries. The features are invariably a strong point, and somehow you tend to focus in on them almost immediately. It's not necessarily the eyes or the hair, it's something else that gives off an incredible feeling of power — perhaps it's simply that Aries ego shining through. You can almost imagine those first words being, 'I'm the greatest, you need someone like me in your life, where have you been till now?' An Aries man is adept at getting what he wants, and he won't wait for it. It must be now or, even better, yesterday!

You can very often guess his sign by his instant approach, the way the eye contact doesn't just stop there. Before too long he's bounding across a crowded room to introduce himself and try to persuade you to leave the party where you've only just met, to go and have a drink in a great little bar he knows down the road. His eyes are shining with enthusiasm and ardour, there will be a wonderful smile that lights up his whole face, his arm will be poised to lead you to the door. You feel like the fairy-tale princess rescued by the knight on a white horse just when your life seemed dull and empty — and off you go.

Naturally that won't always be your first introduction to an Aries man, but from that little example you should find it easy to recognize him. Even if challenges don't appeal to your personality, and you decide to rebuff his overtures, this will make you very much more interesting straight away. An Aries man just won't take no for an answer. His personality suddenly takes on the guise of a small boy refused a new toy by his mother. But that doesn't mean he thinks of women as toys, not at all. Aries is simply a child at heart, he comes into the world saying 'Me first' and what he wants he tries harder than most other signs to get.

So you've guessed this man's sign without much trouble, but it's not always so easy. The more evolved Aries may have learned to hide away certain characteristics, and that women don't always like an instant come-hither approach. Also your dream lover's particular horoscope may contain all sorts of other astrological reasons to explain why he seems more like a Cancer or Virgo. But his head is still usually a give-away. His enthusiasm and ardour are never completely lacking, and wanting something yesterday instead of today is difficult to conceal.

If you've met someone and have a sneaking feeling he just has to be born under the sign of the Ram — but don't want to ask outright since you don't want him to think you're that interested — ease him out gently by getting him to tell you about his work. Ten to one it won't be a mundane occupation. He'll probably say he has a new project just about to take off, and he's sure it has every chance of success. Ask him how long he's been working on it, and he may well tell you he only thought of it a month ago and he's been running like crazy ever since. Dare you ask what happens if it doesn't work out? He will give you a slightly withering look and say, 'I'll move on to the next one of course.' That's a great give-away. Ariens don't dwell in the past, there is always a new challenge to take up, new discoveries to make. If he's not self-employed he'll be using his Aries personality to sell something to someone, and probably be doing very well.

If you still haven't guessed his sign then look at how he's dressed. Aries men may not always be amazingly fashion-conscious, but somehow they tend to wear clothes with great flair, even in the heart of the country. Of course trendy town Ariens are bound to have the latest styles, as they love to create an image from the moment they enter a room. And that Aries head of hair is usually well cut and groomed. There is also a sort of animal energy in the way they walk.

Soon you will realize that you've met someone who is so full of energy, has such a restless quality, and such an attractive personality, that his attention span is probably exceedingly low. And you're right. Aries is looking for excitement, but this doesn't have to mean he's out for a one-night stand and will never want to see you again. Deep down, this fascinating man is as much of a romantic idealist as Cancer or Pisces, living in more of a fantasy world than they do.

He isn't a man who wants to keep changing partners, but the trouble is that once anything in an Arien's life becomes too much like routine, there's sure to be a moment when he feels the need for something new. It might be a very subtle feeling, something so far below the surface that he doesn't even realize it's happening. But if you're determined to keep an Aries dream lover happy you must live up to his ideals all the time — and remember there needs to be good sex too. Once the sparkle starts to go out of a relationship he often cannot cope. It's like those childhood days of wanting something new all over again.

So having learned this much, you'd better make a pretty quick decision as to whether or not you're going to risk the possibility of getting involved from the word go — or whether it might be safer to choose a dream lover with a different sign of the Zodiac!

Having decided you're fearless, where are you going to meet this exciting man? It would be crazy to think that one-twelfth of the population will all congregate in the same sorts of places. Besides, don't forget Aries likes to be different. But if you've started a new job, and you seem to be attracted to a guy who always seems to be on the telephone selling himself brilliantly to the person on the other end; if he greets you with a wide smile when you are introduced and after the compliments he tells you to rely on him to show you the ropes, and you must have a drink after work . . . you've got it. But Arien wolves are plentiful, and he might easily be married with two or three kids . . .

There's no set hunting ground for an Aries man. He probably enjoys sport so you might find him at the local tennis club or squash courts. And with his helter-skelter life he may easily belong to a trendy health club. If a new club or society starts up near you there are sure to be one or two Ariens who pop along to the opening, for this sign genuinely hates to miss out on anything.

If you meet an Aries on holiday it really will be romance time. This man seems to become even more excited about life when he's travelling, but this has its dangers! He may simply be looking for fun, an adventure or passion under the stars, but as he's a pretty sexy man with indefatigable energy in the bedroom, he's not about to divulge his private life to someone he's just met. It's not that he *wants* to tell you lies, for basically he's pretty honest, but with Aries everything seems to be run to deadlines: he fancies you, he wants you, he's determined to have you – but he's leaving for Kuala Lumpur as soon as he gets back to England, and you're pretty sure there's someone permanently in his life back home. Your instinct will have to help you here, for the last thing you want is a quick fling without sufficient thought.

Luckily you already know that the more elusive you can be the harder this man will chase, so keep him at bay as long as you can. With this man it will work, and if you have the patience to wait until he has been to Kuala Lumpur and back, you can be proud of yourself. But of course back home you might even wonder just what captivated you in the first place . . . you never know.

But now let's assume you've really flipped for an Aries dream lover. You're prepared to convince him his bachelor days are over, that he's found the woman of his dreams (even if he doesn't know it yet), and that you'll happily chase rainbows with him for ever – as long as he's faithful. Faithful . . . suddenly you've hit one problem right on the head. Some women who have had an Aries lover or husband seem to feel they were given a pretty rough deal, even if they couldn't always confirm that their men did have mistresses. Aries men always seem to attract publicity with their escapades, real or imagined (Warren Beatty once again, Elton John and Jeffrey Archer). The little child inside Aries seems to get a thrill out of being thought naughty, it's all a boost to that male ego.

Do get it straight from the start. Aries likes to feel free, perhaps not as much as Gemini, Sagittarius or Aquarius, but certainly never hemmed in. Aries likes you to be there when he wants – but don't expect him to be at your beck and call if he has a myriad other things to do. It sounds as though he can be incredibly selfish, but he'd be wounded to the quick if you told him that. He just doesn't see things that way. In fact he's one of the most generous, affectionate, lovable men around. He just has his deadlines, his need to make his priorities paramount, consequently driving everyone else mad when they have deadlines and priorities of their own.

But he doesn't like 'yes women'. He likes his ladies to have minds of their own, and very often careers of their own too – just as long as they're not too obviously more successful than him. It's all down to that ego once again, for although he wants to be proud of you he needs to be the master.

Little things mean not just a lot to an Aries – they're indispensable. To know you've remembered a special anniversary, that you've been kind to his mother when she was feeling low, that you've searched the stores to find him that special red sweater to wear with his jeans, will work miracles.

He loves to use the telephone (but doesn't want *you* calling *him*). Until he's completely sure of you, he may call up a dozen times a day, wanting to know what you're up to, who you've seen, where you've been. It's not just a jealous streak, he is genuinely interested in your life. But with all the things your Aries man likes to do, he may not appreciate it quite so much if you start to follow his example. He wants to be looked after but not possessed, he wants you to be a warm, loving and sexy woman ... but you'd better not adopt his flirting techniques. He wants you there when *he's* there and even when he's not.

He's also aware that he's made mistakes before, for unless he's very, very young, his impulsive behaviour has probably led him headlong into hasty relationships and perhaps even an early unsatisfactory marriage – simply something he was convinced he wanted at the time, but perhaps didn't have the patience to keep working at. Once he's reached his late twenties he will know so much more about his life, and with luck his earlier mistakes won't be repeated to the same extent. His impatience can sometimes grow as quickly as his passion, though, and thus you must not remind him of his past errors. Ariens have an amazing ability to shrug off such things and move on to the next passage of their lives, and if you use the 'I told you so' approach with your Aries man, you may be searching for a new dream lover very soon.

So try to take him for what he is, having learned how to project your own image. You can have great fun with your Aries man. He will love to be the first to try out a new restaurant, and impart his views to all his friends. He will hate holidaying in the same place more than once, and will have great ideas on where to go. Everything has to be new, exciting and different; 'routine' and 'down to earth' are words that don't belong in the Aries vocabulary.

Just think what fun it will be buying him presents. It's back to childhood time again, for after all a typical Aries always is a child at heart. Christmas and birthdays are wonderful times for you to find a myriad gifts: the latest model telephone plus answering machine, a world time clock, or a micro TV.

Perhaps one of the most important things for you to remember is that underneath that dashing, impulsive, enthusiastic, passionate and amusing man is someone who can be as vulnerable as you, and certainly as romantic – but who is not too good at the nitty-gritty bits of life, the boring parts. He wants life to be fun, stimulating, positive; he wants someone who makes him laugh, can be tender, loving and equally passionate in bed; he wants someone who is prepared subtly to keep him guessing so that he feels convinced he's met the dream woman he's been searching for all his life.

Life with an Aries dream lover may not always be easy, but knowing he thrives on challenges, why don't you try one yourself? Whether it lasts for a month, a year or a lifetime, there is one thing certain – you will never forget the time you spend with your Aries dream lover.

☆ THE ARIES WOMAN ☆

If your dream lover is an Aries woman, even though she is ruled by the same planet, Mars, and has many of the same characteristics as her male counterpart, she can still be a pretty different kettle of fish. A woman's emotions *are* different from a man's. There's no getting away from that, no matter if you think otherwise.

An Aries woman will attract you instantly. She may seem to be a whirlwind of energy, a positive fire-ball radiating enthusiasm, but underneath that outward strength there's the same old vulnerability and childlike approach to life as an Aries man. The woman of the species is said to be stronger than the man in this case, although no Aries man would like to hear that.

To capture the heart of an Aries woman you have to zoom in like a rocket and, once assured that there is the right chemistry between you, it won't take very long for her to show she's keen too. She might almost overpower *you* so that you could suddenly wonder what you have let yourself in for!

But if you truly capture the heart of an Aries woman you will have her for keeps – once you have really convinced her that you're the knight on a white horse she's dreamt of since she was five years old. And if your dream lover eventually becomes your dream wife she'll manage to combine the housework and looking after the kids with an interesting (the vital word) job, and still prepare a gourmet dinner.

Don't expect a quiet life with this woman. If you're the sort of man who wants to come home from work, put your feet up in front of the television and sleep – forget it. She may have had an equally tiring day but she'll probably be raring to go still, and two quiet evenings in a row won't be her idea of fun. Romance must be kept alive and so must bedroom antics for this dynamic Fire sign.

Keeping quiet about what's on her mind is also impossible, so be ready for arguments. But she doesn't want a 'yes' man, she wants and needs an equal, or preferably someone who can be stronger than she is.

An Aries woman isn't difficult to spot in a room – she'll probably be chatting away nineteen to the dozen, and you'll notice her eyes, her hair, her make-up, her seductive come-hither look. There will be something about her face you definitely find striking – think of Julie Christie or Diana Ross. If you're any judge of sensuality you'll see there's lots of passion simmering away below.

Seducing this woman may only take a short while if she feels you're right. But you'll have to prove you've got what it takes to keep her interested in your mind as well as your body. The sex side is important, but for her that can become a bore or a chore if the rest of the sparks aren't flowing between you.

If you haven't already guessed her sign, and you've started up a conversation, you can bet this woman will tell you her life history in the first ten minutes, or at least the part she's prepared to let you know. If you have met at a party and it's boring, she'll probably be the one to suggest you move on somewhere else. But don't necessarily take this as a come-on for it may simply mean she enjoys your company enough to want to know more about you, and for Aries there's no time like the present.

She's bound to be dressed in up-to-the-minute clothes. Aries likes to be ahead of fashion, and if not so much as Leo, still up there in the front. Even if she doesn't have a fortune to spend you wouldn't know it. She has a knack of putting clothes together and looking like a million dollars so she stands out in a crowd.

She will seem amazingly independent, as if she's fended for herself all her life. She was born a leader and she's determined to prove it — when she's out there on show at least.

By now you may be wondering if an Aries dream lover is your ideal woman. Are you frightened she's going to take over your life, turn you into simply another conquest? Tell all her friends how she seduced you in three minutes flat? It's true that if you're a sweet-natured guy who'll say OK to anything just to keep the peace, you may find this woman could walk all over you. But that's not what she wants. She's looking for someone who's all man and who can be more aggressive and dominant than her, even though she may not realize it. So having learnt this much about her, you should begin to understand that if you have the strength to tame this woman, you can have a truly exciting life.

But where do you find this fiery creature? Just look wherever there's some action going on. She's so independent she often hates to make her plans too far in advance in case something more interesting comes along. She's on the go from morning to night and never seems to tire. She's the sort of person who'll think it great fun to join a dating agency or put an ad in a lonely-hearts column just to see who might turn up. But equally she could be baby-sitting for friends so they can have a night out, or doing some voluntary work at a local hospital. Ariens may not seem so on the surface, but they are absolute suckers for lame dogs, they care tremendously about other people, and since they are not terribly good with money, are often more generous than their pockets permit.

The Aries woman's likes and dislikes can be as variable as the weather. But if she's set her mind on something, it's difficult to get her off it. She's not as changeable as Gemini, but she certainly has her moments of throwing tantrums about something that only yesterday she might have been delighted with. Normally she likes surprises, but your timing needs to be spot on. She has a great memory for special occasions, and won't appreciate your forgetting to send her a Valentine card − or even worse, bringing her back the wrong perfume when you return from a business trip (especially if she already feels slighted that you didn't take her along).

The Aries woman dislikes being fussed over too much, but hates to be ignored. She wants to be seduced, yet she often plays the role of the seducer. She's a contrary creature but never dull. And though she may hate to admit it, her closest girlfriends probably know that what she is longing for is a strong shoulder to lean on when the going gets really tough. Just don't ever let her know you've guessed her little secret. Aries is a masculine sign, but the people who think this woman is too tough and aggressive often haven't bothered to look below the surface. And if she's tough it's often because she's had to be.

The Aries woman will go anywhere as long as she knows she's in for a good time, within reason of course. Plays, films, concerts, she usually has a wide variety of tastes. And she loves to go on holiday, preferably to exotic sounding places where none of her friends have ever been. That way she has lots of stories to tell when she returns. Never forget Aries is an adventurer, and loves to travel far afield.

When you buy her presents, always look for something original. Don't make the mistake of choosing something you may have bought once before − and certainly never for anyone else, not if she knows about it! She'll love sexy silk lingerie, Krizia sweaters, the latest Walkman, a cordless telephone or a dozen red roses. Let's face it — she loves presents any time and for any reason.

Seduction *is* an art, and seducing an Aries woman can be a wonderfully exhilarating experience, if exhausting at times! It will also be so full of memorable moments that any bad times will fade away so fast you'll almost forget they ever existed.

If you want to seduce an Aries ...
DO
★ Always let your Aries dream lover think *they're* pursuing *you*!

★ Be bright, breezy — and sexually quite irresistible too.

★ Use your mind as well as your body to stimulate this sign.

★ Show you're the independent type, even if deep down you're searching for someone to be dependent *on*.

★ Develop your sense of humour — Aries wants to be amused.

★ Keep your telephone free at peak 'Aries calling times', unless you have a priority involving work.

★ Let your inhibitions go once you're sure this is the dream lover for you — Aries is not the timid type!

★ Learn to be an early riser. This might take practice ... but is probably essential!

DON'T
★ Ever chase this sign, even if you do think you're being subtle!

★ Ever phone them in the middle of a business meeting.

★ Ever tell them what to do — this sign likes to learn from past mistakes!

★ Criticize their best friend in front of them — they're immensely loyal.

★ Get them into bed and then fall asleep right away!

★ Ever tell them lies, even white ones.

★ Ever let routine set in ... boredom is a dirty word for Aries.

★ Expect them to let you finish a conversation when *they* have something to say.

The Taurus Dream Lover

☆ *THE TAURUS MAN* ☆

Are you good at coping with someone who can be incredibly stubborn for no apparent reason? Are you prepared to wait longer than usual to convince a man that his life had been lacking something until he met you? Do you have lots of patience and believe implicitly that what is worth having is always worth waiting for? For Venus, the Goddess of love, rules Taurus, first of the Earth signs, and while it is fairly obvious that this man has his feet well and truly on the ground, she helps him to be a romantic lover.

Taurus hates to make mistakes, he wants to be very sure that you're not out to use him in one way or another. He needs security in all its many forms, and even if he falls for you hook, line and sinker when you first meet, you'd probably never guess. This man isn't usually out for a quick fling (although, of course, there are bound to be some Taureans who won't be averse to this), for no matter where he is from, and whatever his lifestyle, deep down he believes in the sanctity of marriage and a happy home life with a partner who satisfies all his needs.

If you've ever thought that life with a Taurean sounds far too dull and boring, you may be in for a few surprises once you really get to know this man. He's not just romantic, he's pretty sexy too, so don't be fooled by an outward appearance. There could be a multitude of thoughts lurking below that somewhat staid and stern exterior and they won't all relate to practical issues!

Whereas Aries rules the head, Taurus rules the neck and throat ... and if you think about Taureans you know, you'll probably agree that many of them do seem to have a fairly thickish neck, sometimes giving them an almost squarish appearance. And as for the throat, lots of them have pretty good vocal cords: many a famous singer has been born under the sign of the Bull, including Ella Fitzgerald, Bing Crosby and Barbra Streisand. So if you play your cards right, you may be able to throw away that Walkman or compact disc player — you might have your very own singing heart-throb right beside you.

But how do you guess this man's sign? Of course your life will be made infinitely easier if you come across someone who is fairly stocky, with a short neck, warbling an aria from *Madame Butterfly* — but that is a bit like expecting one-twelfth of the population to be exactly the same! However, you should be able to see this man's silent strength showing through, though he may at first appear somewhat uninterested in you. Don't worry, that's part of the Taurean act. Ten to one he's been hurt very badly by at least one woman in his past — remember, he's an Earth man and would hate to put his feet in the wrong place again. He may appear somewhat cool, calm and aloof, but if you're quick you'll probably notice him sizing you up when he thinks you're not looking. And could that have been a fairly sensual look in his eyes? You guessed right but he'll never admit it — not until he's known you a while longer anyway.

Another thing to remember about this man — even if he's interested in you, he may not ask you for a date right away. Things have to build up slowly for Taurus. He may ask for your telephone number if you've met at a party — but if you start to spend your evenings at home waiting for that phone to ring you might be sadly disappointed. And don't expect him to call you at work, for work to Taurus is sacrosanct. It is part of this man's nature, all down to his need to feel secure, and the one way he feels truly secure is when he's earned enough money to build his security on a solid base.

But not every Taurean will have the same sort of personality (although deep down you will always find many of his traits). This dream lover's birth chart might have lots of planets in Gemini – making him far more talkative – or he could have an Aries Ascendant, which would certainly modify his slow approach!

Perhaps one sure way to discover if your sneaking suspicion that this man is a Bull is correct is to get him riled over something, but this is not necessarily wise if you want to see him again! Yes, whoever first coined that phrase about the 'red rag to the bull' did have a genuine reason – and you don't need to be waving something red to see it put into action. You might say with a note of scepticism in your voice that lots of people lose their tempers when something annoys them, but think about it in future. *No one* does it with quite the same panache as Taurus!

But if you're loathe to risk annoying him and ruining the possibility of a future date, there is an easier way to guess his sign. If you've met him at a party and have started off by making polite conversation, it's easy to ask what he does for a living (he's probably asked you first anyway, to see if it's something his conventional personality approves of). If he's an accountant, estate agent, stockbroker, economist, works for a bank or deals in art, then you could be on to a pretty safe bet by thinking he's Taurus. If he seems the artistic type, he might even be a singer, painter or musician, but Taurus doesn't usually get involved in anything which deep down he doesn't feel will make him money. If he's one of the last three you can bet he'll be fairly successful, and you won't have to worry about cold and uncomfortable garrets. Taureans aren't the types to be self-employed either, unless they're absolutely sure of what the current year's income is likely to be – and the next two years too. You've also probably read that Taureans have 'green fingers', so if this man says he's a market gardener you'll have hit the nail on the head when you ask if he was born between April 21 and May 20.

Are you still having a hard time working out his sign? Start to look at his clothes. He's not always the trendiest of souls, as his clothes must be made to last, and he's not impressed by fancy labels (unless they're a name he respects). He wants value for money, styles that won't go out of date. But interestingly enough he's quite a connoisseur when it comes to fabric. The feel of the cloth is vitally important: nothing that feels rough or looks as though it would fall to pieces after it's been cleaned or washed just a few times will be acceptable. His hair will be well cut and probably won't be too long, unless he's one of those more artistic Taureans. His aftershave will smell expensive, and if you get to know him well you'll discover he's quite a sensuous man who doesn't mind spending his hard-earned cash on pampering himself.

If you're good at being patient, and you've now discovered this new man is indeed a Taurus, you may as well start waiting. Don't make the mistake of initiating your next meeting, for this could make him feel you're just angling for an invitation to dinner, because you know he loves good food, usually in the gourmet category. Of course, if you're a gourmet cook yourself, you could let it slip that you're having some friends to a dinner party on Friday week (never make it too soon!) and would he like to join them. But don't be surprised if he declines. He has to be sure that he wants to see you again, and when he does it's going to be *his* invitation, not yours.

You may be thinking that you've chosen the wrong dream lover. That this man is too hard-headed and business orientated for you, especially if you're the romantic type. But don't get me wrong, this man is a romantic in the truest sense of the word. You've obviously forgotten already that he wants to take his time, he doesn't want to risk making a mistake, now or in the future. And not only is he romantic but he's also pretty passionate too. He may have been a late starter in some things — but probably not with sex. His sensuous taste extends far beyond his aftershave and the right wine with his food. What goes on in bed is highly important to him, but he doesn't want a quick fling and goodbye. He's genuinely looking for his ideal dream lover too, and is prepared to spend all the time that's needed to find her — so you'll have a lot to live up to. Always remember that even though those Taurean feet may be heavily planted on the ground, this man's heart bruises more easily than you would have believed, and with his stubborn attitude to life you won't be forgiven very easily if you do something to hurt him, even if it was said or done unintentionally.

So having discovered that the somewhat boring image you've had of Taurus in the past was misleading to say the least, and that he's the dream lover who has been missing from your life, let's start from scratch and find out where you're going to stand the best chance of meeting him. Of course he may hold one of the aforementioned jobs and you might work in the same place. He might be managing the restaurant where you go with your girlfriends once a week, or you could meet him at a local health club (all that good food means he needs to watch his weight), but being a Taurean he's more likely to be found in the sauna or having a massage than in the gym.

If you meet him on holiday, let's hope that he doesn't live too far away from you, for it may not be until you're home that something really starts. He may be scared of a relationship that turns out to be only a holiday romance, even though his feet might not be quite so much on the ground when he's far away from home! But always remember, he doesn't approve of flirting, promiscuous behaviour, or women who drink too much or make an exhibition of themselves in one way or another. (No more making eyes at that sexy waiter if you've just met a Taurus man . . .)

He isn't looking for the sweet, simpering, little-girl type – he wants a real woman, someone who can be an equal to him in bed and out, and someone he can trust. I've never met a Taurus man yet who hasn't suffered disillusionment at least once in his life, and often it wasn't his fault – there's a reason for him taking time to build up a relationship. He knows that instant falling in love can all too often spell disaster for him.

Something never to forget is that this man is Jealous with a capital J. His opposite sign of the Zodiac is Scorpio, possibly the most jealous of all the signs, and remember that every sign has a little of its opposite within its personality.

But as you've learnt how to project your own image, so you can learn how to understand him. Just think how good it will be to feel secure and loved by someone who will never let you down. Think how happy you'll be to see *his* pleasure when you find him a special gift you know he's always wanted but didn't want to spend too much on – a vintage port, a beautifully bound leather desk diary, a compact disc player, a couple of seats for Pavarotti, a gardening book or a hamper of gourmet delicacies.

This man may sometimes be stubborn, obstinate, set in his own routine, fixed in his opinions, wanting to holiday in the same place every year, but he's wonderfully patient when you're in a panic, he's kind, humorous, often highly creative and, of course, he can be a great lover too.

So don't start to have doubts if your dream lover turns out to be Taurus. Remember that he can be the one man who enables you truly to believe that dreams don't have to be fleeting things. They can sometimes last a lifetime — helped by the right partner, of course!

☆ *THE TAURUS WOMAN* ☆

If your dream lover is a Taurus woman, she's ruled by Venus, Goddess of love, just like her male counterpart. But if you think she is soft and easy to convince that you're her ideal man, you may be in for a shock!

A Taurus woman is perhaps even more stubborn and obstinate than a Taurus man. If she thinks you're right for her, even if *you're* not quite sure, watch out! This woman is determined to get what she wants no matter how long it takes.

She may seem somewhat quiet and even shy at first, preferring to stay in the background if she's with other people. What she's probably doing is sizing up the situation, and even if she finds you interesting she may seem to ignore you. She's not always this retiring, though. Once you've got to know her you'll realize there's quite a smouldering passionate side to this woman, and she can be unbelievably jealous too!

To convince a Taurus woman that she can't live without you, you may have to show her your bank balance. Well, not literally, but remember that Taureans need security and that bricks and mortar mean a great deal more than a dozen orchids or a trip across the Atlantic on Concorde. This doesn't mean that they don't like those things as well, but with her feet so firmly on the ground a Taurus woman has to know her future is as secure as can be.

There is an inner strength in this woman that keeps her going even if she's having a hard time. For although she may seem to be so self-controlled and determined, she's as much of a romantic idealist as anyone else. Because of her immense loyalty to a person she loves she can sometimes be hurt more than you would realize; and her obstinate streak makes it hard for her to admit she might have been wrong about any of the men in her life, especially as she always works so hard to keep a relationship on an even keel.

If you've captured the heart of a Taurus woman, you don't have to worry about losing her, as long as you live up to her expectations and never let her down. If this dream lover marries you she'll always make sure you have a clean shirt to wear to the office, your meals will be ready on time, and it won't take her long to cook the sort of food you've only had in expensive restaurants in the past. You won't have to worry about the house-keeping bills, for she is so practical and good at saving that you'll wonder how you managed before she came into your life.

She'll be happy to sit watching your favourite TV programme with you after dinner, but you in turn will have to listen to her favourite operas (not so easy if your tastes in music are far apart). She'll save you a fortune in household repairs, for she is a great DIY woman, even though it may take her a while to get around to whatever needs fixing.

So how do you recognize this paragon of virtue across a crowded room? You already know she'll be standing in the background, and while she'll be well dressed it's probably in a fairly discreet way – no cleavage for this woman, unless she's convinced enough about her figure (many Taureans have a weight problem) and has decided to dress in a more daring way.

But you'll somehow sense she's quite a sexy lady for there's something in her eyes that draws you to her, and if you get the chance to talk to her you'll realize she knows what she's talking about and won't change any of her opinions just to make you feel good. She's tough enough to stand her ground on anything so don't think you'll flatter her by agreeing with some of her views when deep down you think she's wrong. She's learnt to differentiate between the man who's out for a quick fling and the one who believes that conflicting opinions give two people the chance to get to know each other better.

So if you've decided that a Taurus woman is definitely what you need in your life to make it truly fulfilling, where do you find her? Not dancing the night away in your local disco, that's for sure. It's more likely to be at the local operatic society, or an *haute cuisine* class. She loves gardening, so the nearest plant nursery could also be a good spot to find her. But she's not the sort of woman who likes to be 'picked up'! Don't forget she likes a relationship to start slowly, in the old-fashioned way, so if you have a mutual friend who can introduce the two of you, she'll feel much more secure.

She's not the most energetic of people. On holiday she'll be found lazing around the swimming pool, or enjoying an *après-ski* life rather than hurtling down the slopes.

You're not likely to meet her on a blind date or through a dating agency, unless she has been persuaded to go along by someone more obstinate than her. And if you do meet this way, she'll have a list of questions as long as your arm so she can make sure you're suitable!

Just going for a drink is not her idea of an evening out − don't forget that Taureans have sensuous taste buds -- and if she's sure you can afford it, a French restaurant will win her over far more easily than a pub.

She may seem quite a tough cookie, but Taurus is a feminine sign − and a really romantic one too. This woman loves the feel of pure silk, and to be pampered with perfumed lotions and powders, she will never begrudge spending money on her favourite scents, so you should never lack ideas when it's gift time. Think about a large bottle of 'Joy', a cashmere shawl, dinner for two at her favourite restaurant, or a monogrammed bathrobe.

The seduction of a Taurus woman is unlikely to happen over-night. You might even get to the point of wondering why you're bothering, but when she becomes jealous of the time you've spent with an old flame, when her eyes light up when she sees you with her favourite flowers in your hands, when she finally loses her inhibitions and reveals how warm and loving she can be − you'll realize you've met someone who can make you happy in hundreds of different ways. All your past exploits will seem a million light years away.

If you want to seduce a Taurus . . .
DO

★ Be loyal, lovable and a good listener too.
★ Brush up on some body language techniques − it's definitely worthwhile spending extra time on this.
★ Always make lots of flattering remarks and bolster this dream lover's ego when necessary.
★ Always be encouraging about their work projects.
★ Be there when you're needed, even if it means sitting around waiting for the phone to ring. Taurus is reliable even if slow occasionally.
★ Show you have a very sensual side to your personality − it's up to you how you demonstrate that without coming on too strong!
★ Always check out this dream lover's favourite music and food − you can really score high marks here!

DON'T

★ Seem too eager too early on. Taurus hates to be pushed.
★ Ever give the impression you're just a flirt.
★ Go on about wanting to watch your favourite soap if Taurus wants a cuddle.
★ Start bragging about the love affairs you've had in the past.
★ Upset this dream lover's feelings by saying they're putting on a bit of weight − a sensitive issue this.
★ Be inhibited when slow but sure Taurus shows heated passion in bed!
★ Be indecisive when Taurus *does* decide you're the perfect soul mate.
★ Ever try to rush this dream lover when you're making love.

The Gemini Dream Lover

☆ THE GEMINI MAN ☆

Are you up to date on what's happening in the world? Have you read the latest bestseller, seen the newest movie in town? Are you a good listener, who doesn't mind being interrupted time and time again? Are you someone who is bright, witty and attractive and not only interested in clothes and having a good time?

If you're beginning to lose interest, you're not the right woman for a Gemini man. He needs constant stimulation in his life, and not just the sexual kind. Mercury, the winged messenger of the Gods, is the ruler of this sign, and what Gemini needs above all is mental communication with his partner. The way to capture this man is to appeal to his mind as well as to satisfy his other needs. He must never, ever feel bored.

Gemini is an Air sign, and it truly seems this man's feet are never on the ground. He's the social butterfly of the Zodiac, flitting from one place to the next: he's the perennial flirt, the 'chatter upper' of all time, but a lot of fun to be with, even if sometimes difficult to keep by your side!

The symbol of this sign is the Twins, which obviously accounts for that dual personality that surfaces from time to time. People who've been offended by Gemini behaviour describe it as two-faced or, if they want to be really nasty, schizophrenic. There is certainly a touch of Jekyll and Hyde in most people born under this sign – and not just the males!

Gemini's planet, Mercury, rules the mind. Gemini people are good talkers, often public personalities: Queen Victoria, Prince Philip, John F. Kennedy, Henry Kissinger and Joan Collins all belong to this sign. All that nervous energy can lead to tragedy, though, and both Judy Garland and Marilyn Monroe were born under the sign of the Twins. You don't have to be an expert to identify this sign. Watch the expressive way they use their hands while talking, the way they talk enthusiastically to someone they've only just met. There's no hint of shyness here, or if there is it's amazingly well hidden. They never seem to stop talking, going from one subject to another with the greatest of ease.

This man can captivate you quickly. It's something he doesn't even have to think about. Flirting comes so naturally to him you almost imagine him winking at the nurse who delivered him! He has a youthful energy that never seems to die, but that doesn't necessarily mean he's the sporty type. His fencing is usually of the verbal kind – it's mental energy that this man possesses – but he's not short of the necessary skills when it comes down to seduction. If words don't win you over, he'll soon find another approach, and it won't be too subtle either.

Somehow this man possesses a magnetism that is hard to resist. Even if you don't believe half the things he's saying to you – he has the Irish blarney, the appealing personality of an adorable little boy – before you know it you're hooked, and hurriedly buying the first astrology book you can find to tell you how to cope with the Zodiac's Peter Pan.

If you still haven't guessed his sign, ask him what he does for a living. If he's in the world of communications – a journalist, works in TV, radio or publishing – or is a salesman, teacher, or trying to get into politics, and exhausts you telling you about all the various projects he has on the go all at the same time, you will soon be able to hazard a guess that he's Gemini. Of course, not all the Geminis in the world can have the same jobs. Everyone's horoscope is personal to them – the influence of the Ascendant, other planets, all the different aspects, make a big difference — and here we can only generalize. Whatever this man does, though, he'll be using his mind and his voice — a lot!

Ten to one there'll be a telephone call for him during a party, or he'll excuse himself to go and make a call himself. In fact, he's probably easier to spot at parties than anywhere else, for he's sure to be all over the place, introducing himself to every newcomer who enters the room, and making sure they know everyone else. He's the ideal party guest for he saves the host or hostess a great deal of work!

Whether he's working or having fun, this man is sure to be a snappy dresser. It's not that his clothes will cost a fortune, or even that they're the latest fashion, somehow it's the way he wears them. He seems to know he looks good, even if he is wearing a checked shirt with a pinstripe suit. Geminis love patterns like Prince of Wales checks, or stripes, which are often in greys or navy, never too bright. And whether his hair is short or long, it will be cut in a trendy way. He does not wear jewellery, and if he's really the flirtatious type a married Gemini probably won't be wearing a wedding ring.

But now you've guessed his sign, and want to know more about him, and how to tame his restless quality so he doesn't flit off to someone else. Perhaps if you think again about the planet Mercury, and Gemini's need for communication, you'll begin to understand his personality a little better. Deep down this man isn't averse to settling down — he's searching for his elusive dream lover as much as any other man — it's just that his ideal soul mate is a woman who must satisfy him in mind *and* body. This doesn't mean, though, that she has to be another Gemini. In fact, they could drive each other wild, for who would ever get the last word?

Gemini wants every day to be exciting, as he hates routine. Variety is the spice of life for him, so you'll need to be a skilful lover, a witty conversationalist, a brilliant hostess, a child at heart when he's in a playful mood and, of course, a loving wife and mother. Quite a tall order! But don't lose heart, for even a Gemini dream lover can be tamed — at least a little!

Of course, whether you have learned how to project your image sufficiently to be the right person for him is another matter. So be honest with yourself, and if you've passed the test with flying colours it's time to discover where you can meet this fire-ball of mental energy. It might seem easy – for you could probably find a Gemini just about anywhere that other people congregate. He's definitely not a loner, he's the type to go along to a matchmaking agency, thinking it all a great joke; to accept every party invitation that comes his way; to go on all the works outings; to belong to every society and committee around even if he doesn't take an active part but just likes to keep an eye on the new members.

If you meet him on holiday he'll be the one who's seen five European cities in four days. Don't expect to meet him on the beach, unless it's the very first day of his trip. Sand and sea pall very quickly for this man and he is unlikely to be a sun worshipper. Once he's surveyed the scene he'll be off to the nearest bar – not because he needs a drink but because he'll enjoy talking with the locals. Even if he doesn't speak a word of the language he has an inborn ability to manage somehow.

A holiday romance with him could be just that, and if you start to pressurize him about when you're going to meet once you're both back home, your new-found lover could be off at the speed of light. It's not that he is a one-night-stand man but you must have realized by now that he needs to feel free (just like his opposite sign of Sagittarius). So if his Ascendant is the sign of the Archer or he has a Sagittarian Moon you've got double problems, and you'll need an astrologer to work that out for you!

So if you've found a Gemini man, no matter where, and have decided you're the one woman who can tame his wanderlust, just how can you do it? If you're someone who thrives on challenges (like Aries) it may be a greater one than you imagined, but it can also be a lot of fun. Take a crash course in speed reading so that you can beat him at his own game of knowing everything that's going on.

Let him see you're just as busy as he is (or pretend to be), that your day is crammed with a myriad things, but you'll try and meet him on Wednesday week! He's used to giving out that kind of treatment to women, but he's not going to like it too much when it's done to him in return. He wants you to be independent, to have your own interests, and lots of other friends (it doesn't matter if he likes them or not). The important thing is that he doesn't feel you're too clinging – but he can be jealous too!

While he's not the greatest in the world at remembering birthdays or anniversaries, don't be surprised if he behaves like a spoiled brat if you do the same, and don't ever think he's so self-sufficient he doesn't need your advice or support if things go wrong for him. He does. It's just that he would find it hard to ask – it would mean losing his image – so always do it in a subtle and discreet way if you see he's feeling down, or you know that he's had a rough day at work.

When it comes to gift buying for this man you can have fun. He loves gadgets, subscriptions to new magazines, a new Filofax, the latest Rubik puzzle or the largest crossword you can find – anything that taxes his mind is perfection to Gemini! The latest model telephone, answering machine, or pocket TV is bound to please him.

By now some of you may be thinking you've met a fickle, no-good, selfish guy who wants you when he wants you – and forget about anything else. But everyone puts up a certain self-defence no matter how much they deny it, so why should your Gemini man be any different? Deep down he's probably scared of a serious commitment; he may have seen too many marriages flounder and end up in the divorce courts; or he may come from a home where the constant bickering between his parents made him vow he would never end up like that. Until you really know your Gemini man (and perhaps one never really knows the many different sides of this sign), you shouldn't pre-judge him too harshly.

All relationships need to be worked at, and at least if your dream lover has turned out to be Gemini you know that you won't be in for a dull life – and that is worth a great deal.

He wants a caring, loving partner just as much as other men do, and if you've begun to feel that your mind has to excite him more than your body, don't worry. His sexual prowess won't dis-appoint you, even though you may have to get used to having the most unlikely conversations at the most unlikely times. You have to remember he sees nothing wrong in making love to the woman in his life and managing to think of other things at the same time. It's certainly not that he thinks any less of you.

Living with a Gemini dream lover will have its share of ups and downs. You may sometimes be irritated beyond words by his failure to live up to some of your ideals, but if you've come this far you know you wouldn't be happy with a life so full of daily routine that you sometimes hated to face the morning. This way you have a man whom you may never completely tame, but who will also continue to surprise you in one way or another. And if he does forget your birthday, is that really such a big deal? In return you'll have a dream lover who can make you laugh with his witty stories, call you up on Friday afternoon to say you're flying off to Paris for the weekend, and who shows his immediate appreciation when you've tried out a new and flattering hairstyle.

Isn't it worth putting up with his sometimes childish behaviour, his flashes of temper when he thinks you're not listening? He may not be a saint, but he'll make your life a constant adventure, and be a loving partner when he's found the soul mate he needs.

☆ THE GEMINI WOMAN ☆

If your dream lover is a Gemini woman, she has the same planetary ruler, Mercury, planet of communication, as her male counterpart, and this woman needs mental communication to make a relationship work just as much as the Gemini man.

So if you're the strong silent type, who still thinks a woman's place is to be seen and not heard, then you'd better give up before you even start with this female! You might be the greatest lover since Casanova, but you have to have something in your head other than sexy thoughts with which to stimulate her. You have to be the kind of man with whom she can discuss her most profound thoughts, even if it is 2 am after a passionate session of making love.

But then you'll remember how you fell for her that very first moment you met. It may have started off badly, she made it plain she disagreed with what you'd said, and probably came up with all the right reasons as to why you were wrong! You weren't used to women getting the better of you in an argument, and you weren't sure you liked it. Then you realized just what a bright and vivacious personality this woman had, how she manged to make everyone else around them seem dull.

Of course, if anyone turns out to be dull, it might be you – if she lets you get away with it. A Gemini woman can't put up with being bored, not even for an evening – unless, of course, she's fallen for you so heavily that she doesn't even notice your faults, and that would definitely be against her character, so forget it!

This woman can make your life more exciting than you've ever known before, as she won't seem to behave the same way from one moment to the next. But she does use up an incredible amount of nervous energy, and Gemini women don't always have the easiest of lives emotionally (Marilyn Monroe, Judy Garland and Joan Collins once again), possibly because they simply don't understand that they have this deep inner need for a man who can equal them mentally as well as in bed.

Still, if you're able to win the heart of a Gemini woman and persuade her that you're the partner she's been dreaming of all her life, you'll have a woman who will keep you happy both in bed and out. Of course there may be days when the housework doesn't get done, she forgets you've invited the boss and his wife over for dinner, or even forgets to pick up the kids from school because she's engrossed in a telephone conversation with a friend she hasn't seen for years. But what is life if it doesn't contain a few surprises?

Isn't it great to know that her bad moods will never last long; that the tenderly romantic woman lying beside you can turn into a passionate sex-kitten the very next moment; that her many questions don't mean that she's trying to check up on you but that she is simply genuinely interested in what you've been doing since you went off to meet the boys? If she ever goes through your pockets it will probably only be to see if there's any spare cash around to pay the milkman because she forgot to go to the bank before it closed. She doesn't have time to be jealous, there are so many other things on her mind most of the time.

However, if your eyes lit up at that last remark, don't think you'll have *carte blanche* to play around and that she won't care – she will! And if you remember that 'hell hath no fury like a woman scorned' you'll be on the right track. You'll get it all verbally and more! Gemini may be called two-faced and deceitful – often unfairly – but it's something they find hard to accept in anyone else!

If you've met someone new and haven't yet guessed her sign, even though she hasn't stopped talking for ten minutes flat, look at her appearance, her ability to mix colours and patterns and not look a mess; the way her make-up and hairstyle enhance her, making her look even younger than you're sure she is. She will have an admiring audience around her, yet may suddenly look at her watch and say she has to rush off to meet some other friends.

If after reading all this you're still keen to try and meet Ms Gemini she may have placed an ad in the personal columns, be president of the local debating society, work for your local radio station or travel agency, be a receptionist or air hostess – anything where she's going to meet lots of different people all the time.

She's the kind of woman who loves surprise presents (like Aries she's a child at heart!). Try a subscription to her favourite magazine, a telephone answering machine, a few videos for the bedroom. She likes surprise outings too.

She doesn't appear on the surface to be the kind of woman who can easily be seduced, but if your brain matches your brawn you'll find it a fascinating experience! She doesn't fit any of the usual descriptions of 'the little woman', but she's a woman with a big, big, heart and a wide variety of interests, the more the merrier. Variety isn't just the spice of life for her, it's one of life's greatest necessities.

Let her pick your holiday spots. She's great at finding somewhere off the beaten track where there will still be plenty of night-life and lots of shops to browse around so you can find her the sort of original gifts she loves.

If you've often dreamed of meeting a woman who can hold her own in male company without being too bossy, of a woman who can create excitement from the most mundane experience and who manages to keep smiling even in the most difficult times, don't look any further. Practise your most seductive smile, catch up on the latest gossip and international news − and start searching fast!

If you want to seduce a Gemini . . .
DO
★ Try to be as scintillating out of bed as in.
★ Be knowledgeable about what's going on in the world even if it means getting up an hour earlier to read all the papers.
★ Be an ever-attentive audience to your dream lover's words (even if you sometimes yearn to get a word in yourself).
★ Give the impression of being fascinating, fun-loving and fancy-free as a companion (even if you have other things on your mind).
★ Be a mental turn-on, remembering that Gemini's most erogenous zone is the mind!
★ Be a constant challenge, and perhaps sometimes a tease too!
★ Be as flirtatious as your Gemini dream lover (easy if you happen to be Gemini too).
★ Be interested in your dream lover's life without ever being nosy!
★ Be a good friend as well as a dream lover!

DON'T
★ Ever be possessive.
★ Ever be a bore (worse than being possessive).
★ Expect a Gemini dream lover to remember everything you say.
★ Make sex the be-all and end-all of your relationship, there has to be much more with Gemini.
★ Try to lay down any rules − they won't be kept.
★ Ever put down your Gemini dream lover's latest craze, even if you know it won't last.
★ Be shy about experimenting with a few bedtime games.
★ Ever be too available − keep that Gemini interest burning.

The Cancer Dream Lover

☆ THE CANCER MAN ☆

Are you ready for a man who can be tender and loving one minute, and inexplicably moody the next? Can you deal with a man who wants a woman who is mother, wife or mistress, depending on how he feels? Would you be irritated if the dream lover in your life turned out to be a better cook, and certainly more domesticated than you?

Ruled by the Moon, the Cancerian moods fluctuate like the tides. A Water sign, Cancerians are so sensitive that lots of astrologers in the United States have taken to calling them 'Moon Children', so you can imagine that if you upset their feelings they'll soon start scuttling into their shells without a backward glance!

Perhaps the most important thing to remember is that his mother has to approve of you, or at least to think you can improve under her wonderful son's guidance. Lots of people tend to think it's only Italians and other Latin men who have a sort of mother complex, but don't kid yourself. Cancer men of every shape and form, no matter where they come from, have an incredibly strong rapport with Mum. There's certainly nothing Oedipal about it, but if you fall for a Cancer dream lover, no matter whether his mother is around or has passed away, you'll have to live up to what she expected his woman to be!

If you want to capture and hold on to this man, and you're not too domesticated, you'd better take a fast crash course in how to make healthy and nourishing food. If you've started to feel despondent, thinking you'll be chained to the kitchen sink whilst all your friends are out having fun, don't worry. This man doesn't want a skivvy. He is a wonderfully romantic lover who is so instinctive he'll know just how to please you most. His emotions are bottomless. When he truly gives his heart he really does want it to be for keeps. Not only can he be quite a sexual athlete between the sheets, but he is the sort of man who loves to kiss and cuddle and sit dreamily beside you in front of the fire on cold winter nights.

If you've often felt that a Cancer man could give you the sort of contented domestic life you've always dreamed of, you could be right. But how will you recognize him?

If the maxim that the way to a man's heart is through his stomach (the part of the body ruled by Cancer) fits anyone better than a Cancer man, I'd like to hear about it. Yes, I know that Taureans love good food, but somehow Cancerians seem to have that rounded appearance to their middles that helps you to recognize them. Of course this is a generalization, for while Henry VIII fitted that description, Ringo Starr obviously doesn't. The face of a Cancer man can sometimes be a give-away also. It may be slightly moon-shaped, with soft, sensitive eyes that seem to know what you're thinking before you've even said it.

But he's not a softie. Inside every Cancerian there's a tough-ness and practicality which you'd associate more with his opposite sign of Capricorn (but then there is invariably some-thing of our opposite sign in all of us).

Of course, if you meet this particular dream lover when he is going through one of his rough patches, and he appears to be taking his bad mood out on everyone around, check in your diary. If it's full Moon time it's bound to affect him, for the Moon rules his sign. 'Lunar madness' tends to create more mayhem at full Moon time than at any other. It's even been said that some doctors don't like to operate during the full Moon.

But don't over-react. No one is suggesting that your dream lover is going to turn into a werewolf. It's just that as the Moon affects the tides, so it has a strong effect on Cancerians as far as their feelings and emotions are concerned. So if you feel that this man is ignoring your presence, even being slightly rude, don't take it to heart. He could be quite different tomorrow or the next day.

It hasn't been too difficult to guess this man's sign, has it? If you're still floundering in the dark, you'll have to try another approach. Ask him about his work. Once again, like his opposite number Capricorn, this man can be a real workaholic. The careers you might find him in are hotel management, teaching, social work, antique dealing, estate agency or veterinary surgery. Cancerian men are also good in banking. In fact, they're usually good at whatever they've set their heart on doing, as long as the ambience is right. But the Cancerian dream lover can be extremely reticent at telling you too much about himself until he's got to know you, so you might have to work on a different tack.

Look at the way he's dressed. He can't be called slovenly but he's hardly Mr Fashion Plate. What he wants is to feel comfortable, whether it's relaxing in front of the fire at home with a pipe, or going to the office. On the whole he prefers sloppy casual clothes – which can also hide a multitude of sins around his midriff! His hair may be floppy, but Cancerian men often seem to lose their hair earlier than some of the other signs. When they do it gives them even more of a moon-faced appearance.

So what have you got? A man who loves his mother, good food and domestic bliss, and who has a highly practical streak and plenty of skill as an attentive and highly emotional lover. He is also one of the most loyal and supportive partners you could find.

This man understands what it is to feel lonely or rejected, for his sensitivity has sometimes led to incredible shyness in his earlier years: perhaps he was bullied at school for not being a whizz at sports, or because he always had to run home when the other kids were hanging around the playground. So if you're going through a tough patch yourself, he'll always comfort and protect you, cuddling you in his arms to let you know you'll always be safe with him. He's a real romantic, this Cancer man, so isn't it worth putting up with a few crabby moods? (Besides, once you become used to them they won't seem nearly so bad.)

If you've decided that you have to have a Cancer man with whom you can sail off into the sunset and live happily ever after, where are you going to meet him? He usually loves the water, whether it's pottering around in boats, sailing in a really serious way, fishing in your nearest river or stream, or simply walking the dog along the seashore.

The problem is that this man isn't usually terribly sociable. You might even meet him because he's the son of your mother's best friend, and she's longing for him to meet the right person. This can be helped along by your own mother singing your praises in the best possible way!

If he's a divorcee, and has custody of the kids, you could always offer to take them out one day – once you've got to know him, that is – for if they take instantly to you it's sure to be a huge bonus in your favour.

If you meet a Cancer on holiday you're in for some real romance: long walks hand in hand in the moonlight, murmuring sweet nothings to each other while the crickets chatter and a romantic ballad drifts from a distant taverna. Somehow the Cancer man seems to unwind on holiday and is more inclined to let himself go. You'll discover he has a great sense of humour that you will find immensely appealing. But be careful – you may not even suspect that he can be moody at times, for he's thoroughly relaxed. And if there isn't a full Moon he may be a perfect gem every day!

However, it won't take you long to realize that he likes to have a woman dealing with the little things in life: telling him that colour shirt to wear and even picking the colour of his socks. Cancer men do like to be mothered, although some would hate to admit it!

So what happens once you've used your best seductive skills to make this man fall head over heels for you? You've even agreed to meet his mum and know just what you're in for. You've put up with a few black moods, and you've gone through his good and bad points a million times in your head.

If you're the sort of woman who wants to continue with a career, take care. This man is sure to want to be a father sooner rather than later. His romantic dream of perfect domestic bliss is to have a home full of kids when he gets home from work. Mind you, he won't be so happy if they wake him up with their cries in the night, or climb into your bed when he's trying to have a lie-in. He'll expect you to make sure they're well-behaved, although he may spoil them excessively!

But the good points will outweigh the bad. You couldn't find a more loving father than this man. He has incredibly deep paternal instincts, and his warmth and sensitivity make children of every age adore him, for he also understands what it's like to be shy and nervous (especially when the first day of school comes along).

Still, before you get to the children stage, you'd better remember that whilst your Cancerian dream lover possesses a wonderful sense of humour − when he wants to turn it on − he's also possessed of a strong jealous streak. Perhaps jealous is a slight exaggeration, but he's certainly Possessive with a capital P, and if you ever give him cause to think you're playing around with someone else, beware. The Cancer man builds a nest for a lifetime. He hates to think of things like divorce, especially if there are children involved. So if you've made the mistake of falling for a married Cancerian and he has fallen for you, try to understand what it will mean to his conscience if it means breaking up a home. If your love affair turned into something more serious, he might end up feeling guilty all his life.

Because Cancer is such a sentimental sign, little tokens of affection mean not just a lot, they're *essential* to him! So always remember to put special words on your cards, to spend longer than you expected on finding him the perfect gift − a barbecue for the garden, an antique decanter, a bedside coffee or tea maker, a soft cashmere sweater, a warm woolly dressing-gown for those cosy winter evenings together by the fireside or a storm lantern or new fishing rod for the Cancer fisherman. And always, *always* remember his mother's birthday!

What you must remember above all about your Cancer dream lover is that this warm, generous, compassionate man really does believe in the rainbow's end and a life that can be happy for ever-more. He isn't a playboy (well, I'd have to look at his horoscope to be completely accurate on that!), and domestic bliss is something he'd go to the ends of the earth to achieve. Why not let him see he doesn't have to go as far as that — if you're still sure you can live up to his ideals? And once you've learnt to put up with the days when he's like a bear with a sore head, you'll realize that while life with a Cancer dream lover will have it's fair share of ups and downs, you'll also enjoy the comfort and security of knowing you have a very special man about the house.

☆ THE CANCER WOMAN ☆

You've spotted her across a crowded room, and she blushes when she realizes you're staring at her. Yes, even in today's world there are Cancerian women around whose cheeks go red when they realize they've been singled out for attention! But of course you don't know her sign yet!

If your dream lover turns out to be that Moon-ruled Water sign of Cancer, at least you know you'll always eat well! She's probably been baking cakes and biscuits since she was tall enough to reach the kitchen scales!

A Cancer woman will make you feel comfortable almost instantly. She has a warmth and sensitivity that many of the other signs seem to lack. But even if she also tries to come across as tough, it won't take you long to realize it's all a great big act, for underneath her shell she's often incredibly insecure.

While writing this book in the Algarve I became friendly with a Portuguese Cancerian woman who told me she felt Cancerians are just like containers — that they take everything inside them-selves — and certainly most Cancerians I have met do seem to take on everyone's problems. Cancer might be a Water sign but the Cancer woman is a real Earth Mother, and sometimes she has to be forgiven for hiding away in that shell. There are moments when she needs to cut off from the world, to recharge her batteries and get back into the right frame of mind to tackle the rest of the day.

To capture this woman's heart it's no use trying to sweep her off her feet with a great line in chat — she'll see through it instantly. Never forget that after Scorpio and Pisces she is one of the most intuitive around. If she thinks you're just out for a good time, her shyness will disappear as she cuts you off with a mouthful of carefully chosen scathing remarks.

You need to go slowly with Ms Cancer because she likes to be wooed in a more old-fashioned way. No, it's not that she's prudish and cries 'rape' every time a man tries to touch her, she's just a true romantic who, at the right moment, will certainly show you she enjoys good sex as much as the other eleven signs of the Zodiac. But that right moment has to grow on her, and she has to know you're genuinely keen.

If ever there was a woman who puts up her defences a million and one times a day, it's this one, but once she's yours you may wonder how you ever survived without her!

If your dream lover one day becomes your wife you need never worry about not having a clean shirt for work, or eating proper meals. She wants to look after you in the true sense of the word. But the only snag is that she can sometimes become overly possessive, smothering you with her love, and it's hard to explain to her that you're not a little boy. To Cancerian women, men of all ages need mothering, and sparks can fly if you're a man who has been fending for himself for years.

It's not that she's jealous, but if you ever give her reason to think you've been unfaithful, you'll soon change your tune! She just needs to know that you would never let her down.

If you haven't yet guessed this woman's sign, having talked to her for half an hour, it's no use being fooled into thinking that Cancerian women are always soft and cuddly. No, they can be up-to-the-minute fashion plates like Princess Diana and Jerry Hall, two Cancerians who've managed to combine their social and domestic lives so well. On the whole the Cancer woman isn't overly extravagant with her clothes, for she's the sort who spends money on feeding her family and waits for the sales to come around before she splashes out. You'll notice she likes very feminine clothes, so that can be a clue to her sign. But unlike the two famous Cancerians mentioned above, many born under this sign tend to be fairly well-rounded.

Are you getting panicky about that 'little mother' bit? You don't need to, for if she learns early on not to fuss over you too much, she won't make the same mistake twice. And she's not *always* prepared to be 'the little woman at home'. Cancerians may be skilled home-makers, but they're also good at whatever they put their minds to. There is an inherent practicality within this sign, and a strongly creative streak too. You'll have a partner who is equal to you in more ways than one if you decide on a Cancerian.

She will be wonderful with children too, although once they start to grow up she'll have to let go the reins a bit. Cancer mothers tend to be overly protective, and this can lead to too many arguments around the home.

If you've decided you have to meet a Cancer woman, where should you start? She could be a nurse or social worker, a job in which she's involved with caring for people, or she may be teaching or involved in an archaeological dig (she's a great lover of history).

Her likes and dislikes will depend on her mood! She loves to be surprised with a huge bunch of flowers, or dinner for two at her favourite restaurant just to take her away from the kitchen for once! She is also probably even more sentimental than her male counterpart when it comes to cards with the perfect message inside.

The Cancer woman loves to be fussed over from time to time, and she deserves it. She appears to be so capable even when she has the worries of the world on her shoulders, and she's the sort of person others have probably taken for a ride many a time.

Whereas Aries comes into the world saying 'Me first', Cancer keeps quiet but feels a great deal − perhaps more than any of us will ever know, for the Cancerian feelings aren't given away easily, not after her emotions have been bruised a few times.

This woman loves romantic films and books, dinner parties with friends, holidaying by the sea or taking a boat on the canals. But she's a homebody at heart, needing her loved ones around her − she doesn't need to travel to exotic places to feel fulfilled. And when it's time to give her a gift − just make sure you give it with love. It doesn't have to cost the earth, or be the most original present in the world, for with Cancer it's the thought that counts more than anything. She might appreciate things like a Victorian locket, your grandmother's pearls, a silver photograph frame, a couple of romantic novels, a pasta maker.

It's also the thoughts behind your actions that count when it comes to seducing a Cancer woman, so if all you're after is one night of passion forget it. Love and sex must blend together in the right amounts, and when they do it's magic.

If you want to seduce a Cancer...

DO

★ Develop your sensitivity, and be warm, tender and loving (mother, father, psychiatrist all in one).

★ Practise being patient (not easy for some of you).

★ Be supportive in every possible way.

★ Be a homebody more than a social butterfly (some acting lessons could come in handy for some of you here).

★ Be a good cook, or have enough money to eat in restaurants where 'Mamma' is the chef: home cooking is the way to this sign's heart!

★ Show you'd be the perfect person to cuddle up against on a cold winter night.

★ Be sensual without being overpowering – caresses achieve a lot with Cancer.

★ Be emotional and sentimental – and always remember anniversaries.

★ Always show you're a romantic at heart.

DON'T

★ Ever tease this sign too much – Cancerians over-react.

★ Get too close at full Moon times if those famous bad moods are apparent.

★ Be a spendthrift – Cancer is more practical than you may think.

★ Ever flirt too much if you want to captivate this dream lover.

★ Come on too strong – Cancer isn't looking for a boss.

★ Waste this sign's time if all you're looking for is a flirtation — Cancer *really* wants to settle down.

★ Be a prude — Cancer's not so shy beneath the sheets.

★ Ever play around with anyone else just because you hope to snare this dream lover — it will have a truly negative effect.

The Leo Dream Lover

☆ THE LEO MAN ☆

Are you prepared to worship a man as though he were a king? Can you be a loyal, loving and willing subject to this regal ruler's whims? Do you find it easy to sit back and let someone else give the orders? Does singing praises (even when you doubt it's justified) come easily to you?

Leo the Lion is the second of the Fire signs, and without doubt he is the King of the Zodiac. Ruled by the Sun, this man radiates sunshine, and immense power too. He's not the sort of man to trifle with unless you happen to be another Leo and can roar and rage as loudly as him!

He's more of a hunter than Aries, but equally as romantic. Even Cancer and Pisces would have a hard job matching his romantic idealism when he's found the mate he wants to snare. By his law of the jungle, once he's found that mate, woe betide anyone else who tries to intervene — the lion's territory is his for keeps.

Leo's birth dates coincide with summer time, when the Sun is at its zenith. This is when Leo comes into his own, needing the sun perhaps more than most of the other signs. Grey rainy days seems to cast a shadow on his personality as he needs the brightness of a clear summer's day to feel totally alive.

And, of course, he needs to be in love! He might be one of the strongest signs around, but he's a child when it comes to love. The lion becomes a pussy cat, purring contendedly, his roar forgotten. Leo relates astrologically to the heart, and when this man *gives away* his heart (metaphorically of course), he gives it for keeps — if you can live up to his expectations!

Leo is also one of the signs that relates most to show business. Think of Alfred Hitchcock, Danny La Rue, Mick Jagger, Madonna and Sean Penn (two Lions together, no wonder those sparks always fly). The Princesses Margaret and Anne were both born under the sign of the lion.

Have you fallen hook, line and sinker for a man whose personality seems to radiate charm, who gazes at you as though you were the only woman in the world? Look at his hairstyle (unless he's reached an age where he may have lost most of it) — doesn't it somehow resemble a lion's mane? Does he have a beard? Believe it or not, of all the Leo men I know, most of them are currently sporting beards, or have grown them frequently in their lives. No matter whether they're English, American, Italian or Portuguese, I can think of at least six this very moment!

It's almost as if a Leo enters the world convinced he is king, and everyone around is expected to be a courtier. His first cries probably even sounded like roars when he wanted to be fed, for even the babies of this sign hate to be kept waiting for anything, let alone refused it! And if his mother wondered why that sunny little face suddenly scowled when strangers looked into his pram, it was probably because he felt they weren't praising him enough!

So if that handsome bearded man with a smile that lights up his whole face bounds across the room to ask your name, and in the same breath says he's bored with the rest of the crowd and why don't you and he go somewhere else, you've guessed it right — he's Leo! But of course not every Leo man behaves or looks exactly like that. You probably know enough about astrology to be aware that someone's personality also depends on the time and place they were born, on the Moon, Ascendant, and placing of the other planets in his horoscope. But I'd still defy anyone to show me a Leo who doesn't want to be boss!

But if you've recently met someone who doesn't exactly fit any of my descriptions, yet you've a sneaking suspicion he has to be a Lion, try to glean his sign without really asking; find out whether he likes going to the theatre, or if he's seen any good films recently. For whilst every Leo can't be in show business, most of them love the associated glitter and dazzle, and take a great deal of notice of what's going on. Your next half hour might be taken up with showbiz gossip. You're on pretty safe ground now if you want to ask nonchalantly if his birthday is in late July or August.

Or you can draw him out about his work. If he doesn't tell you he runs a company or is trying to take one over, he is sure to have some kind of managerial position somewhere. If he talks about it all with enthusiasm, yet doesn't seem to be the sort of man who'll stay in the office late if there's something entertaining on the evening's agenda, you'll feel even more secure and prepared to hazard a guess. But Leo careers include acting, film directing, fashion, heads of companies, PR and theatre management.

And if even now you're still in the dark as to his star sign, look at his clothes. No matter how much he earns, Leo has to look a million dollars. He's the status symbol collector of us all (as is his female counterpart), and would rather have one item from Gucci, Hermes or Giorgio of Beverly Hills, than half a dozen from a manufacturer whose name doesn't mean as much. It's not that he's a great snob, he just honestly feels better if he's wearing something that comes from a well-known designer, so he never begrudges the cost (often more than he can afford). Leo is one of the most extravagant signs around.

It's not just the clothes he's wearing that can attract your attention. This man *knows* he looks good, and just as the lion of the jungle possesses great magnetism and strength, so does his namesake. You can almost feel he's sizing up his prey, ready to pounce on what is usually a willing victim! That wonderful smile which lights up his whole face, the way he dominates the gathering, is irresistible. He's the king searching for his queen, so you've found yourself a 'real' dream lover!

It won't take you very long to realize that this man wants to be treated like a king from the word go. It's the one role he feels is rightfully his. If you decide a Leo dream lover is for you, let him boss you around a bit, remembering that underneath he's a

114

cuddly little cub who only wants to prove he's got you tamed the way he wants. And flattery and compliments mean a lot to him — as long as he feels you mean what you say!

Have you decided that this is the one man for you? And that you're quite prepared to be at his beck and call (within reason, of course)? Do you feel he's the most warm-hearted, friendly and generous man you've met for a long while, and that it's wonderful to be with someone who is obviously proud to be with you? If until now he has only existed in your dreams, where should you start to look for him? Wherever the sun is shining for a start! Or at least somewhere where he has a chance to shine himself. He's a party lover, and a great host, and he might be the leading light of your local dramatic society. If he likes sport, he could be showing off his style at the tennis club. There's no set place for this man, but it's always where the action is — unless he's having one of his lazy days. Even though he's one of the Fire signs, the Lion likes to relax too, perhaps more than you'd expect.

If you hope to meet a Leo on holiday, you'd better be prepared to save up for a really first-class, preferably a luxury, one! Leos aren't likely to stay in little *pensiones* unless they know they're absolutely unique. They expect more than ever to be treated royally, and whether it's the sea, lakes or mountains, that sun had better shine above. If you *do* meet him on holiday, you're in for a lot of fun, and one of the most romantic times you've ever know. The art of seduction is important to Leo the Lion, and you can bet your life that if he's gone on holiday alone, he's looking for a dream lover too. On holiday he can let his hair down and not think about work.

If he really falls for you, you'll have one of the most attentive lovers you've ever known. But woe betide you if he catches you flirting with somebody else. This man has to be boss in and out of bed! However, he's not averse to chatting up someone else himself — and of course, as you've probably guessed, he won't like it if *you* tell *him* off! What's sauce for the goose is not sauce for the gander with Mr Leo!

But don't start to get worried, a Leo who finds the right woman is unlikely to stray very far. Don't forget that he wants to receive love just as much as he loves to give it. If he's really sure about your feelings for him and he feels the same way about you, the king of the jungle doesn't usually look for another mate.

Although he likes to be bossier than most, the one thing he doesn't want is a lover who is permanently in awe of him — he likes strong women, as long as they're not stronger than him. He admires independence in others, as long as they realize that they also have to come when he calls! He may seem selfish at times (he isn't really, for he's definitely one of the most generous men around), but his pride simply won't let him take second place. He has to be the dominant one in everything and only if you're a Leo woman can you really hope to tame him. So don't try to beat him at his own game, and always let him feel you're proud to be with him, unless of course he does something so awful that you have every possible reason to roar yourself.

This man has a heart of gold, he'll give you everything he can — and he loves you to do the same for him. He loves receiving little gifts, they don't have to be *too* expensive — for it's really the thought that counts with him — but you could try some Giorgio cologne or a champagne bucket with his favourite champagne! To know you love him enough to remember the anniversary of the first day you met; to give a surprise party with all his closest friends when he receives an important promotion; to buy tickets for a musical he's been longing to see . . . these things all mean a lot to Leo. Of course, if you can afford it, it's true that he loves to wear gold, for this is his colour and his favourite metal. (For the man with everything how about a gold-plated toothbrush?)

But sometimes you may come across a Leo man who seems strangely subdued, and if you can't help wondering why, put it down to love, because Leo can't cope with being rejected. If he's had a disastrous love affair with someone he felt he'd have conquered the world for, his heart will be badly bruised, and it will take a long while for him to recover. You could, therefore, have a hard time convincing him you wouldn't let him down. Never pry into his past because, as he's such an open man, he'll tell you everything he wants you to know, and you should leave the rest alone. Once you have his trust and never let him down, he can be yours for keeps.

You might be wondering if, once a Leo dream lover has settled down into a steady relationship, he will become even bossier, expecting to have his own way over every single thing. (It's certainly true that this man is hardly ever a hen-pecked husband, but then if you've gone as far as living with him he's unlikely to ever become that, or your bags would have been packed for you long ago!) You don't have to worry, for if he's truly happy his roar won't be heard nearly as much. He'll still be the same wonderfully romantic lover you first fell for, and you'll never be bored with his playful antics in the bedroom.

But you'll have to play *your* part too. Never forget he always wants to be proud of you — the woman who captured his heart. For just as he likes other people to admire him — he wants them to admire you too. After all he feels *he* picked *you* out, so even if you know deep down it was your own seductive arts that lured him into your den, that's one little secret you should keep for ever and ever.

Life with the Leo dream lover can sometimes be exasperating, especially when he gets into one of his ultra-bossy moods; or when the bank manager calls to say your joint account is way into the red, and you know full well it's not because of you; or when he calls you up at 5pm and tells you he's invited an important colleague and his wife over for dinner that night. But with Leo the Lion, your life will never be dull, and it will be filled with lots of sunshine and a great deal of love. What could be more important than that?

☆ *THE LEO WOMAN* ☆

Think of Jackie Onassis, Madonna, Princess Margaret, Princess Anne, Lucille Ball and Susan George. There's no way anyone could describe any of these as the kind of woman who is seen and never heard! So if your dream lover is a little 'yes woman' who worships the ground you walk on every single moment of the day, you'd better forget all about seducing a Leo lady. Or at least that's how it may seem at first. But don't be taken in by this woman's domineering ways, for the best way to win her to your side is to boss her around a bit. She can be too forceful for her own good, and deep down she knows it. She'll often welcome a man who shows her he's the boss, just as long as she respects you and you remember to give her praise when it's due.

Your Leo woman is ruled by the Sun, and obviously has many of the same characteristics as the Leo man, radiating a sparkle when she enters a room. Her hair may be almost more mane-like the Leo man's, for there's usually a lot more of it. It often tumbles about her face, in carefully calculated disarray, although never too untidily for that would detract from her regal appearance. This woman has great sex appeal — and she knows it.

She has to be the star turn, the centre of attraction. The limelight was made for her. Let other people stay in the chorus, Leo ladies like Sarah Brightman know they have to be right up there in front.

So to capture this woman's heart she must not only respect you, but you'd better be the master of the game when it comes to love — and sex! She won't put up with selfish lovers, so you'd better make sure your technique is up to scratch.

But if you're beginning to think you're likely to land yourself with an arrogant, demanding shrew, you've got the picture all wrong. Just like the Leo man, this woman's heart is very big, her roar may seem loud but under the surface she's just a cuddly pussy cat who wants to be loved.

Try to understand it's not easy to be a Leo woman, second of the Fire signs. She is always described as being strong, forceful, dominant, bossy, a leader amongst women. Sometimes it's truly hard for her to tone down her personality, for giving orders comes much too easily to her. She was probably the leader of the pack when she was a tiny child — and the picture has never really changed. What she wanted she somehow managed to get. Yet gains scored too easily soon mean very little to her, which is why she often has such a hard time with men.

The Leo lady loves to be in love — it's essential for her to feel really fulfilled. The trouble is it's far too easy for her to lose her heart to someone because she's fallen for his appearance and he's been incredible in bed. It's a bit like going for status symbol clothes. A man who looks good and dresses well, who takes her to all the right places, has learned one sure way of seducing this fiery woman.

But to truly capture her heart you've got to have something more: you've got to have stamina to last the course; brains to match your brawn; and you have to order her about (not too much), just enough to let her see that *you're* the boss.

If your dream lover ends up your partner for life, she's the kind of woman who'll put everything she's got into making you happy. She'll be a wonderful hostess and her parties will be the talk of the town. She'll be a very loving mother (although when the children start to grow up she may have to get used to stepping out of that limelight slightly more).

If you can't guess her sign by her hair, or her fashionable clothes (which have the Italian or French designer stamp down to the heels of her shoes) you're sure to feel the force of her personality. This is one woman who is quite likely to seduce *you* if you haven't been quick enough to do it first! For don't forget she has no qualms about going all out for what she wants. This woman is a huntress, and if you're her prey you're in for an exciting time.

So where do you find her, if she's not working in some high-powered position in the same business as you? She's a tough career woman, an accomplished actress, a great PR consultant, and wherever there's a party or swinging disco in town, you're sure to find a Leo. She works hard and plays hard too. She loves anything remotely linked to show business. She adores holidays in sunny exotic climes, where she can be treated as a queen, of course!

If she's the hostess of a party you're invited to the perfect gift to take along is champagne, preferably vintage. Leos love receiving gifts in all shapes and forms – a Louis Vuitton bag, Armani jeans and expensive French perfumes – but you mustn't despair if your bank account won't allow such extravagant gifts. It's very much the thought behind the gift that counts with her. (But if you *can* afford it, remember that Leo loves gold – gold bracelets galore would be very much appreciated!)

Seducing a Leo lady may seem like a difficult task, but it's worth it in the end, for you'll end up with an incredibly loyal and loving mate – once you've tamed some of her more dominant ways, of course. Just make sure you never let her know you realize she's not as tough as she pretends to be. She wants to be respected for her strong personality and treated like a queen – that's a Leo's birthright after all.

If you want to seduce a Leo . . .

DO
★ Think up as many compliments as you can (fake a few if necessary), as Leo has immense pride!
★ Show that beneath your admiring glance beats a warm and passionate heart.
★ Be sparkling and dynamic. . .as long as Leo appears to be *more* so.
★ Make sure you have a great sense of humour.
★ Always let Leo be the leader (or at least think that's the case).
★ Let this dream lover see you can be a pleasure-loving partner in more ways than one!
★ Always let Leo be the centre of attraction (even when you feel it's *your* turn), at least until the seduction game is won!
★ Help your Leo dream lover achieve success and recognition – it will show how much you care.
★ Wish for the sun to shine continually (Leo would be yours for life if you could achieve this one).

DON'T
★ Boss your Leo around (although they don't like complete subservience either).
★ Criticize your Leo dream lover, especially in public – just think what it would do to their pride.
★ Ever let Leo feel you're the better lover of the two of you (it's all down to pride again).
★ Criticize the Leo extravagance – if they can afford to spoil you, at least enjoy it!
★ Forget that lions can be playful but want a fiery sex life too.
★ Let this dream lover feel neglected, and never, *ever* stand them up.

The Virgo Dream Lover

☆ THE VIRGO MAN ☆

Are you good at taking criticism? Are you prepared to get involved with a man who seems to worry about every little thing, has pernickety tastes about his food, and thinks he's going to die of Asian flu when he gets a cold? Of course I'm generalizing, but I do speak from personal experience when I say that Virgo men aren't the easiest in the world.

Virgo is 'the sign of service', and don't they know it! Ruled by Mercury, the planet of the mind, Virgo is the second of the Earth signs, and Virgoans have a fantastic ability to analyse and discriminate, hence they become such strong critics. They can't help seeing faults, but on the plus side they're able to notice the good points too!

If you can live up to the expectations of a Virgo man, you can have blissfully happy relationship. He's not the kind to play around with other girls. He's invariably a one-woman man, and believes in the sanctity of marriage and the family. If, for one reason or another, he does end up divorced, he tends to feel guilt, even when it's not his fault.

If you've met someone who doesn't appear to be really shy, but somehow leaves a great deal unsaid, never forget that while

Virgo may criticize others, he does the same to himself. He often undervalues himself, and if you're the sort of person who has a bright and breezy personality, even if he's violently attracted to you, it may take him a while to pluck up courage and ask you out.

He's a great stickler for detail, and again tends to worry incessantly if he feels something is not quite right. Peter Sellers is a great example of someone who was brilliant at his craft, but seemed to be constantly insecure, and Greta Garbo hates to be seen in public. There is great sexuality hidden beneath the apparent coldness of Virgo, revealed in the writings of D. H. Lawrence and on the screen by Sophia Loren.

When you've met a Virgo you will often be struck by the precision of their features, every detail may remain in your memory. They may not be handsome or beautiful, but they will be striking.

One of the first things to remember if you're hoping to snare a Virgo dream lover is that he usually hates to be pursued. He is sure to think there's an ulterior motive. He may be slow but he's definitely sure of what he wants and it's wise to wait for him to make the moves for otherwise you could scare him off and spoil what might be a wonderful relationship.

So if you've met an interesting man, who seems rather cool and distant on the surface, but there seems to be quite a lot going on beneath, he could be a Virgo. Even on his 'casual' days, a Virgo man dresses with impeccable style. But no idle follower of fashion is he, in fact he doesn't even particularly care about fashion. He just wants to look neat and tidy, from his haircut down to his toes.

You'll soon discover that Earth-ruled Virgo definitely has his feet on the ground when it comes to practicality. Like those other two Earth signs, Taurus and Capricorn, he doesn't fling his hard-earned cash around – even when he's practising the art of seduction! If you've met someone who has some of the above attributes, but not all of them, don't forget his own individual horoscope could mean he has the influence of some more lighthearted signs, for obviously I can only generalize here.

So if you're still playing the guessing game – and fear he'd look down his nose at you if you started to talk about star signs since he seems much too cynical and sceptical to believe in the art of astrology – try to draw him out about his work. Virgoans are often accountants, book-keepers, theatre critics, or in publishing, nursing or medicine, and they tend to stick in the same job for years (living up to that description of being 'the sign of service'). Often they take jobs that would seem boring to other people, but they seem to thrive on routine. They're not always terribly ambitious, and can be difficult to work with because their colleagues feel they have a lot to live up to.

If a dream lover starts to complain about the cigarette smoke drifting his way, or the draught from an open window which is making his neck ache, you are safe in thinking he is a Virgo. Of course, he might well be smoking himself *and* blowing it all in your eyes, but it's OK for him. Perhaps that's unfair, but I really can think of one or two Virgo men who've been just like that. And heaven help you if you're driving with him and you open the passenger window and let too much air inside!

It won't take you too long before you decide you've met a somewhat complicated character. However, the lovely thing about Virgo men is that while they're masters at criticizing other people, they genuinely do recognize most of their own faults, and some of them are indeed far too self-critical.

Perhaps this is where you come in. If you've discovered your dream lover is a Virgo, and are wondering with fear and trepidation if you have met with his approval – you'll soon know if you haven't. This man doesn't believe in wasting time! And if you feel you're with someone who sometimes fails to enjoy the best moments in life by worrying too much, you can look forward to helping your new-found Virgo to relax.

Where should you look for this man if he's not slaving away at the desk next to yours at work? Sport isn't really a typical Virgo hobby, unless it's criticizing McEnroe's behaviour on the TV screen. He could be quite a highbrow type, found at a debating society, or casting an analytical eye over the latest exhibition at the local art gallery. He's unlikely to spend much time having drinks with his mates; Virgos aren't great drinkers, they're against anything that they feel could be bad for their health.

If you meet him on holiday, he may be the man complaining

about something at reception. In the hotel restaurant he's probably eyeing the menu with caution – none of that nasty foreign food for him, thank you very much. But you have to realize that it's all because he may have led a sheltered life, or been brought up by parents who encouraged his fussy ways. For even tiny little Virgoans make it known early on that they're fussy about their food, and if they were ever left with a dirty nappy their howls would make someone think they were being ill-treated!

If anyone needs to unwind on holiday it's Virgo, so if you meet an unattached man born under this sign, you could help him discover a new side to his personality. He isn't looking for a purely holiday romance – in fact he probably looks askance at couples who are enjoying just that. And it's going to take more than a few days before he first asks you for a date, so let's hope you're blessed with plenty of patience.

Virgo may be slow at the outset where passion is concerned, but he's a pretty nifty lover once he's made up his mind that you're the woman for him. There are two sides to everything, and romantically he can be a real winner. However, don't be surprised if he makes a few critical remarks about your own particular techniques (if you're forewarned, you can have a few sarcastic quips up *your* sleeve).

One thing you'll have to remember with this man, is that if he's had his heart broken in the past, he'll be loath to make the same mistake again. Perhaps that's also one of the reasons he seems to sum you up so deeply – he wants to be really sure he's not going to end up hurt. For although it is Scorpios who are supposed never to forget, you can often say exactly the same for Virgo, and a broken heart often seems to leave Virgo criticizing himself even more bitterly, therefore becoming more insecure.

Perhaps that's one more reason for him to take his time in making that very first move, to the point where you honestly feel he's not interested. Then just as you've given up and decided that the Virgo dream lover is not for you – he'll surprise you and ask for a date.

Still, don't get me wrong, life with Virgo is definitely not boring, it's just that it sometimes takes longer to reach its most exciting moments. Once you've captured his heart, though, and he knows you're not simply a fickle flirt, things can be a great deal of fun.

He's a man who remembers everything — it's stored away in his head and he probably doesn't need a Filofax. You'll never have to moan that this man forgets your birthday or the anniversary of your very first date. This means, of course, that you'll have to try and do the same yourself (it's expected of you), so if you're a disorganized sort of woman, you'd better mend your ways fast! He expects you to remember things that mean a lot to *him*, and even though he may not seem like a great romantic, forget to send him a special card on St Valentine's Day and you'll be in trouble!

You've found a great protector in this man. While you sometimes wonder how you'll cope when he gets into one of his hypochondriac phases, it's nice to know that if you're not well and have to spend a few days in bed, the Virgo man will look after you wonderfully, tending to all your needs, without a single complaint. This man really enjoys looking after people.

Never push the Virgo man into doing something he's not happy about, for he'll display a very stubborn streak. And he's not going to be too keen if you start criticizing *him*, not until your relationship is well under way at least.

If you're planning a special treat, make sure you don't pick a restaurant without being sure he'll enjoy its particular cuisine — for remember he's the sort of man who imagines he'll end up with a tummy upset after eating anything too rich. When you buy him presents — something to wear is always a good idea — it may seem to take you for ever to find something he will really like. He certainly won't want you spending too much or being frivolous in your choice. He hates extravagance, as he works hard to make money and he hates to think of it disappearing in a flash. But some things to think about are a desk organizer, a battery operated stress meter, an ionizer and humidifer, and the latest software for his computer.

One of the things you must never forget is that whilst Virgo may appear so discriminating and analytical, he's just as capable of having a good time as any other sign. He just needs to be drawn out more. He *can* be incredibly passionate — you won't have to complain about your sex life − but you'll have to let him think he's taught you everything you know. Virgo is the sign of the Virgin, but this man is no shy little boy when it comes to the art of love.

Convincing a Virgo dream lover that you're the perfect mate for him isn't going to be easy, and at times the way he criticizes you will make you feel as though you're back at school. But his assets outweigh things like this, and you'll appreciate his tender loving gestures a million times more − and realize that the real thing is even better than the dream!

☆ *THE VIRGO WOMAN* ☆

If your dream lover is a Virgo she is in good company − Greta Garbo, Sophia Loren, Lauren Bacall and Twiggy all belong to this sign. And you'll soon find you have a lot to live up to in order to convince her you're the perfect mate.

A Virgo woman may bring a new kind of challenge into your life. You won't be able to get away with some of your old tricks − she'll see through them instantly − and she won't have to be an astrologer or clairvoyant to know what makes you tick. She's just as discriminating, analytical and critical as her male counterpart − perhaps more so, because she uses her feminine intuition in the strongest possible way.

She may attract you because 'Virgo' makes you think of purity, but this woman can be just as impulsive as Aries, as flirtatious as Gemini and certainly as provocative as Scorpio, sex symbol of the Zodiac. Even if she is somewhat prim and proper when you first meet, she'll prove to be a ready, willing and more than able mate, if there's a mutual attraction.

If a relationship with a Virgo woman develops into something deep and lasting, you won't have to worry about her straying. Virgo is the second of the Earth signs, and Virgoans have a deep and abiding loyalty to the people they love, which is why it's important not to let them down. A Virgo who has been betrayed finds it very hard to have complete trust again. She may go so far, but if she feels she's set off on the wrong path again, she has an uncanny ability to end the situation, however unhappy it makes her feel.

You may not have a very easy life with a Virgo woman if you're the kind of man who's never picked up a duster or folded your clothes before crawling into bed. Virgoans of both sexes are perfectionists. Everything has to be just so, neat and orderly. And even if this woman is totally besotted with you and swears undying love, she'll still expect you to do your bit around the house.

If you've often wondered what a Virgo woman would be like how are you going to spot her? In a crowded room she's sure to be the one eyeing everyone else up and down when she doesn't think they're looking. You can almost hear her mentally criticizing their appearance − in the nicest possible way of course! But she'd probably blush and deny everything if you decided to tackle her with it later on. If you draw her out in conversation, she's sure to have very definite views on every single topic and if you disagree she'll probably prove that her powers of analysis are greater than yours.

Look at her clothes. You won't find her shoes need cleaning, or an uneven hem on her skirt, and while she probably won't be wearing way-out designs, it will be obvious she has a keen eye for fashion and knows better than most just how to mix and match.

She will also seem a lot more independent than she is. A Virgo woman can sometimes be somewhat awesome, for you feel she knows so much more than you. It can be disconcerting to feel you're under a microscope when she first gazes into your eyes. You may find it hard to imagine her as a carefree lover, as she looks as though she's the kind of woman who is determined to keep her emotions in check. You might even be wondering if a Virgo dream lover is the right one for you, fearing that she'll start comparing you to lovers she's had in the past, and putting you way down the list. But once you've got to know this woman, you'll recognize that, beneath that critical exterior, she's not nearly as tough as she seems.

So where should you look for your Virgo dream lover? Since you probably already know Virgo is known as the 'sign of service', you'll realize she has a strong sense of duty and can be found wherever there's work to be done. She is the kind of person who comes into the office early and ends up leaving late. So if you meet her at a party it's probably on a Friday or Saturday night when she can take it easier the following day. She may be doing voluntary work at the local doctor's surgery or hospital, browsing over reference books in the library, or baby-sitting for friends, at a yoga or gym class, or at a health club.

Her likes and dislikes are not difficult to imagine. She's fussy to the point of obsession about certain foods and she probably dislikes men who drink too much and make a spectacle of themselves. She's also embarrassed about great shows of affection in public, but when you're alone she's quite prepared to let herself go. And she loves to be surprised with little unexpected gifts, or cards with a meaningful message to let her know she's always in your thoughts.

Just because she often seems cool and distant, it doesn't mean she doesn't want to be seduced. It's just that with a Virgo woman the art of seduction really *does* have to be an art. Virgo is a feminine sign and this lady is all woman when she wants to be.

If you want to take her somewhere special, she loves good plays and films; she's very culture conscious and has probably read far more than you. On holidays she'd probably get bored lying on a beach for too long, and she's not usually the disco type. Give her stimulating company, good food, and with the right man around, she'll even forget her critical ways.

When you're buying her a present buy her a sweater with a sexy neckline instead of the more severe styles she tends to buy for herself. Be generous, treat her to a week at a health farm, or give her a juicer so that she always has fresh orange juice to hand. Get some satin sheets for the bedroom – or extravagant silk underwear that she'd never buy for herself – and let her know she's more than just a dream lover, she's the wonderfully warm and loving woman you've waited for all your life.

If you want to seduce a Virgo . . .

DO

★ Be perfect in every way (or at least seem as if you are)!

★ Be emotionally strong (you'll need to be for those days when Virgo criticizes everything you do).

★ Establish yourself as a good friend before too much seducing takes place (however, this may depend on the individual Virgo concerned).

★ Be prepared to understand that Virgo can be fussy to the point of paranoia . . . about everything.

★ Be cool, calm and collected . . . and inwardly pure!

★ Make it obvious you're not playing the field — Virgo is not usually a playboy or girl.

★ Be appreciative and complimentary about how hard they work.

★ Be intellectually this sign's equal — there needs to be a true blending of the minds.

DON'T

★ Get in on the criticizing act yourself (hard if you're the same sign).

★ Ever persuade Virgo to eat anything they're not happy with — not even if you're hoping for an aphrodisiac effect.

★ Undermine Virgo's confidence in any way — sometimes their insecurity could sink a ship.

★ Ever say anything derogatory about their love-making — it's one of the things Virgo takes great pride in.

★ Ever fool around with other people, even if it's only faked to create attention.

★ Moan if this dream lover has offered to help someone out when they're supposed to see you. Remember that this is the 'sign of service'.

★ Embarrass Virgo in public, in private it can be bad enough!

★ Ever forget an important anniversary, this sign remembers everything.

The Libra Dream Lover

☆ THE LIBRA MAN ☆

Charm personified — that's the understatement of the year where this man's concerned. Ruled by Venus, Goddess of love, Libra is symbolized by the Scales, and many Librans spend an inordinate amount of time balancing things up before making a decision, which is why so many people call them indecisive!

If you've set your heart on a Libran dream lover, and he has set his heart on you, don't worry about him being indecisive, he'll make his move just as quickly as any other sign. He may be an Air sign but he'll also prove he can be just as fiery as any Fire sign.

Of course, it may sometimes seem as if he takes for ever to make up his mind to ask you out, but he has to size you up and make sure your personality will blend with his. He's a real connoisseur is the Libran man and nothing but the best is good enough for him. It's not that he's snobbish, or has set ideas of what he wants, it's just that his sense of the romantic is highly attuned, and subconsciously he has his minimum requirements — for deep down he's searching for a dream lover too. Librans, perhaps almost more than the other signs, have a basic desire to find the perfect partner and certainly don't like to be alone for too long.

The Libran man has definite style, and more often than not he has the looks to match. Think of men like Roger Moore and you'll know what I mean. And no one can doubt that Librans have great creative talent: think of John Lennon, Sting, Anthony Newley and Harold Pinter.

But how are you going to recognize this debonair, charming, creative man? Perhaps it is the almost lazy way he flirts with you, although not just with his eyes or the way he speaks... He may not noticeably generate as much sex appeal as Scorpio, but you can tell he's all man and that he's not just interested in your mind alone. He seems to gaze at you in a gentle, caressing way and you feel the understated sensitivity in the way he draws you out. He's rarely the brash and arrogant type, unless he has some conflicting characteristics in his own personal horoscope (and you'd have to check that with an astrologer). However, you can tell he could be a womanizer by the way he notices every pretty girl walking by – not in an obvious way, mind you – and in fact it's often so discreetly done that you might even miss it!

If you don't have much knowledge of the Libran man, and feel you may have just met one at a party but didn't like to ask his sign, one giveaway could be his lounging lazily on a couch while you, and everyone else were standing. Librans hate it when they're accused of being lazy, and indeed some of them are extremely energetic, but they're often the exceptions rather than the rule! If somebody suggested moving on somewhere else, and this particular man seemed to take longer than anyone else to make up his mind, then he was most likely born under the sign of those Scales.

One note of warning, Libran men like peaceful lives, and if you're the sort of woman who tends to argue incessantly, even when you know you're in the wrong, you'd better find yourself a dream lover born at a different time of year. Libra is the sign of peace and harmony, and this man finds quarrels very unattractive. He'd sooner walk away than find himself involved with someone who tries to pick a fight just because he doesn't agree with her. So even when you know you're right about something, point it out with care.

However, if you've met someone very appealing, and still

haven't been able to work out his sign, why not try to draw him out about his work? Ten to one it won't be anything too energetic. Librans often tend to gravitate to the more artistic fields. Obviously not every Libran is going to be an artist, poet or musician, but they do make good diplomats and lawyers, and their creative flair may draw them to hairdressing. Of course his own particular birthchart may be full of planetary aspects that lead him into a totally different career, in which case you will have to try again.

Have a look at the way he's dressed, for now you should definitely be getting somewhere. Whether he's in casual or work clothes, there's sure to be an elegant and debonair look about him. Somehow he seems to have great flair in the way he wears his clothes. He's not particularly narcissistic, but if there's a mirror around you'll probably catch him taking a peak just to convince himself again that he is one of the most attractive men in the room. Another thing about him, of which he's gleefully proud, is that he always manages to look younger than his age. I can think of one devastatingly attractive Libran in his early fifties, who doesn't look a day over thirty-five and of course he knows it!

Once you've become involved with a Libran dream lover, you'll discover life can be a real delight. He's the perfect lover, and if you thought Scorpios were the sex symbols of the Zodiac, don't be surprised if this man shows you more than a few tricks of his own! He's definitely not the sort of man who after making love falls instantly asleep and starts to snore. He likes to cuddle up to you, and to be sure he's pleased you before falling asleep. He's just as loving and attentive when he's woken up by the strident sound of the alarm clock in the morning — as long as it's not too early, for he's not always too good at rising at the crack of dawn. Librans have to have their beauty sleep if they're to keep those boyish looks!

But while this man doesn't set out to be a Casanova, there's no doubt that he has an eye for a pretty face, and if you ever let him feel neglected once you've captured his heart, an idle flirtation with someone new could turn into something more. However, he does not like a jealous woman hovering anxiously over him: you'll have to be adoring but cool as well, not too easy if you happen to be a more passionate and fiery sign. And he certainly won't care for the idea of your indulging in a little flirting yourself. He may be all for equality in most things, but not when it's a case of his woman chatting up another man.

If you've never been involved with a Libran man before, but quite fancy the idea of meeting one, where you start to look for him can prove quite a poser. For since he's not normally the energetic type, you can forget about tennis courts or football games (unless he's an avid spectator), although, of course, with his sense of fair play he'd make a perfect umpire. No, cricket or golf could be more his style, as long as the weather is warm enough. You might come across him in a unisex sauna, or with a group of friends at the local disco, looking wonderful in his latest casual gear.

Because Librans love company so much, you're not likely to come across one wandering along the beach on his own. He could be sitting chatting in the local pub with his friends, or lying on a beach soaking up the sun. Which brings me to Librans on holiday – and this is when the Libran dream lover becomes even more romantic. It might take him for ever to make up that indecisive mind on where to go, but sunshine is a must, as is good food and a really comfortable bed. He's the sort of man who likes to eat in small restaurants, serenaded by a gypsy violinist playing the most romantic pieces in his repertoire.

Somehow Libran men seem to become even more sexy when they're away from the routine of everyday life. So if you actually meet a Libran dream lover on your package tour to a Greek island, you'll have a wonderful time looking at sunsets together. Forget the sunrises – he'd rather stay in bed even if you haven't had a particularly late night! You'll love the way he tenderly wakes you up with a kiss, and gives you a happy smile. The Libran dream lover was probably the sort of child that gurgled happily away in his pram while other babies were bellowing their little heads off. He learned from an early age that being sweet and love-able brought the most rewards and he's certainly carried those lessons well into adulthood!

But do you think you can cope with the sort of man that other women may flirt with? Would you subconsciously shudder every time you saw him eyeing a beautiful bare-breasted girl on the beach? Are you prepared always to be as charming to his friends as he is to yours?

Are you better at balancing the budget than he is? For this man isn't necessarily practical. In fact, he can be extremely extravagant when he wants to be, and he's also the sort of man who has forgotten to go to the bank just when you need some extra cash.

Still, his eye for beauty does mean he'll always pay you wonderful compliments, he'll notice the way you arranged that vase of flowers, and sniff appreciatively at the new scent you're wearing. He's also the sort of man who is wonderful with kids, even though that sometimes means he can be rather too easygoing when discipline is required.

Libra wants a balanced partnership, so he won't complain if you're a real career woman – as long as deep down he knows he's not going to take second place in your heart. And if you're wise you'll never let him think otherwise.

He loves to be spoiled on birthdays, anniversaries and at Christmas. You don't have to spend very much, it's the delight of opening the gifts that gives him pleasure. And it's not hard to find presents for the Libran man – a pullover to match the colour of his eyes, his favourite aftershave, a Liberty silk scarf, some designer ties, an electric drinks mixer – and at least one card telling him you adore him as much as you did when you first met.

What he doesn't like is to be nagged. He'll get on with things in his own time, and if that doesn't suit you, perhaps you'd better choose a dream lover born under a different sign. And don't ever be pushy and domineering, or expect to captivate him overnight! This dream lover doesn't mind how long he spends looking for his soul mate. He knows he wasn't born to live alone, and with Venus, Goddess of love, helping him along in the romance stakes, you can bet he'll find her before long.

It's up to you to project your image in the best possible way to keep this man by your side. For once he's sure you're right for him, he'll do all he can to make you happy, and you're unlikely to regret having him by your side. Just make sure you keep the romance alive in your relationship, for if life becomes too mundane his eyes could start to wander, and your dream lover may not seem quite so perfect after all! But if you want a man who can charm the birds off the trees, is romantic and tender and who can be the perfect partner in so many ways you could certainly do a whole lot worse than finding yourself a Libran.

☆ THE LIBRA WOMAN ☆

If your dream lover is a Libran woman, then count yourself a very lucky man! While I was writing this book, someone asked me which sign I thought was the best, and although normally I hate questions like that, without any hesitation I found myself saying Libra, not even knowing that the questioner was one herself!

The male and female of the species may have the same planetary ruler — Venus, Goddess of love — and many of the same characteristics, but the Libran woman feels and thinks quite differently from the Libran man. It's almost as though she works harder than anyone at creating the really perfect partnership when she's with the man she loves.

With the Libran dream lover you're immediately attracted to her femininity and that soft but sensual air. She usually has impeccably good taste, artistic qualities and quiet loving ways that will make her a pleasure to be with. She's definitely quite a catch, but you'd better be warned right now that it often takes quite a while for her to decide on the right man to share her life.

The Libran woman is usually never short of willing partners. She never has to do the chasing, which might seem quite rare in these liberated times. But then she has infinite faith in her sexuality, her charm and her ability to captivate the man she wants. The art of seduction is so skilfully played by Ms Libra that you probably haven't even noticed it. If ever there was anyone better at waiting for that telephone to ring, I'd like to know about it. She's the sort of lady who might not even answer in order to make you think she's out on the town the night you've said you'll call her. An Aries or Gemini couldn't manage that!

If you are determined to try and capture the heart of a Libran woman, you have a lot to live up to. She's no snob, but she does have her requirements. If you think about some of the ladies born under this sign you'll realize there are some formidable names amongst them: Brigitte Bardot, Britt Ekland, Julie Andrews and Sarah, the Duchess of York. They're certainly not little 'yes women', and each one radiates that Libran charm in her own particular way.

One thing they all share is that they obviously believe totally in their ability to charm the people they come in contact with. They never lose their femininity even if they are hard-working career women or ardent feminists. Another wonderful thing about Libran women that you'll soon discover is that their symbol of the Scales gives them the ability to weigh up the pros and cons of everything, to take a balanced view, and let any verbal attackers say what they want without getting into an argument about it.

You may have begun to feel, though, with a Libran woman spending so much time sizing you up and debating as to whether or not you and she could make beautiful music together, that the end result could only prove disappointing. But how wrong you'd be, as you must not let her gentle, sensitive Libran exterior fool you when it comes to love and sex. She will surprise you if the time and place is right. It's just that it probably has to be in *her* time – she will not rush into a love affair at the drop of a hat. She wants to know you better, to learn your likes and dislikes, to make sure you're not trying to seduce her just to chalk up another victory for your own sexual prowess.

The Libran woman isn't usually out for passionate adventures that lead to nothing in the end. It's not that she's trying to trap every man she may fall for, but whether she knows it or not, she really is looking for a lifetime partner.

Another intriguing thing about Libran ladies is that when a marriage or long-standing relationship comes to an end, for all her sense of feeling somewhat incomplete without the right partner, she is able to pick herself up and cope without losing her balance. She isn't the sort of woman who panics and creates dramas, more often than not she's able to shrug her shoulders and say philosophically that, although she may not feel too great inside, there was right on both sides and it was just one of those things...

So you've met someone who is sweetness and light personified, but you're still not sure about her star sign. She gives away a lot by the way she's dressed. Somehow she has the knack of making almost anything look wonderfully feminine and sexy without having really tried. It's as though her Libran balancing act enables her to find colours and styles that blend and harmonize perfectly, and the result is 'all woman'. Unless you've met a particularly unusual Libran, she won't be dressed in anything too flamboyant or provocative, nor anything too demure. She strikes the happy medium and her make-up is skilfully applied to blend perfectly with her outfit. She has wonderful fashion sense, and you'd better not be too scruffy yourself, for it definitely won't go down well with her.

Perhaps you are beginning to worry that you've met someone so critical that she's going to make you change your life completely. However, she's definitely not as critical as Virgo, it's simply that she has an artistic flair and wants to see beautiful things – and why not? Besides, almost more than any other sign this woman really does put everything she's got into making a relationship happy for both parties concerned. She's not going to keep picking at you for little things unless they really do create problems between you.

And the lovely thing about her is that you feel she needs the support and encouragement of the perfect dream lover to make her feel completely whole (all due to Libra being the seventh sign of the Zodiac, which relates to partnerships).

If you've decided that what you need more than anything else is a Libran woman in your life, where should you look? She's the sort of person who likes to relax listening to music or talking to interesting people; she loves to laze on the beach or enjoy an evening at a disco where the music isn't too loud and brash. Librans tend to be where other people congregate. She often browses round art galleries, goes to concerts and, of course, loves holidays where she can really cut off from the hustle and bustle of everyday life.

Present-buying for this woman is a real treat..She enjoys being spoiled – and she will appreciate pretty scarves, jewellery, LPs of her favourite romantic singer, silk or satin lingerie, anything by her favourite designer, some labour-saving gadgets for the kitchen.

But you'd better think carefully about your seduction techniques with Ms Libra – she might be weighing up your every move – and if you want those Libran scales to tip in your favour, the soft, slow, sentimental approach will probably work best.

If you want to seduce a Libra . . .

DO

★ Be kind, understanding and make your personality as attractive as you can.

★ Be prepared to be the decisive one when it reaches that should we/shouldn't we moment.

★ Always let your Libra dream lover feel you need their advice about something, it flatters their egos (and they're so good at putting the balance back into your life too).

★ Show that you're interested in the arts – most Librans have a pet painter or favourite piece of music.

★ Make sure you share a calm, peaceful and relaxed life.

★ Pamper your Libran dream lover in every way possible.

★ Show that you're the sort of person who loves to have a relationship on an equal footing.

★ Let your Libran dream lover know from the start that you hate arguments as much as they do.

DON'T

★ Ever tell a Libran he or she is looking older – this sign takes too much pride in keeping young!

★ Force Libra into making an important decision if it really is against their will.

★ Ever chase this dream lover too much if you're not getting a reaction, for this sign finds it hard to tell you you're wasting your time.

★ Keep on about how lazy Librans are supposed to be.

★ Ever accuse your Libran dream lover of being fickle – you could drive them to it!

★ Ever let your Libran dream lover feel you're only out for a good time.

★ Turn up looking terrible if you've managed to get that first date — Libra has an eye for beauty always.

★ Be anything less than the perfect lover, at all times.

The Scorpio Dream Lover

☆ THE SCORPIO MAN ☆

Me Tarzan, you Jane! Of course, not every Scorpio man will come into your life by swinging down from the branch of a tree, flexing those muscles in front of you so your knees go weak. But this man probably knows he's often described as the sex symbol of the Zodiac, and feels he has to live up to his macho image. Ruled by two planets — Mars, God of war, and Pluto (in Greek mythology Hades, the lord of the underworld) — poor Scorpio is one of the most maligned signs of the Zodiac, often unfairly so. Everyone talks about 'the sting in the Scorpion's tail', and yet I can think of several Scorpio men who have remained incredibly loyal friends through thick and thin.

Scorpio is a Water sign, though you could be forgiven for thinking that his sexual techniques remind you more of Fire! He's a lot more sensitive than you may give him credit for, and if his feelings are wounded it's hard for him to forget. It's sometimes said that he doesn't forgive easily, but that's not such a problem for him, it's the forgetting that can be almost impossible.

He has incredible inner strength, which is why so many astrology books describe him as invincible — and on the surface he is. It's not that he has two personalities, but he's adept at hiding a lot of what he thinks and feels. One of the most instinctive and intuitive signs of the Zodiac, to the extent that he almost seems to read your mind, he also has a jealousy and possessiveness that is sometimes hard to take, especially since the last thing *he* wants is the same kind of behaviour from you!

Scorpio likes to delve deeply into life — its mysteries fascinate him but sometimes he becomes so intense that more matter-of-fact people tend to back away. If you've met someone whose animal magnetism frightens yet fascinates you, if the brooding quality of his eyes holds a fascination you've never felt before, and if you're prepared for a passionate and life-enhancing relationship with someone who is definitely all man, then he's the perfect dream lover!

Some fascinating men have been born under Scorpio — Picasso, Richard Burton, and Prince Charles — and your very own Scorpio dream lover can be fascinating too provided you learn to outsmart him at his own game.

Have you wondered how you will recognize this dazzling man? I don't believe you'll have very much trouble. Those eyes for a start are often the greatest clue: he really does seem to peer into your very soul when he's practising his inimitable art of seduction.

If he's attracted to you, he'll probably have no qualms about making his intentions very clear from the start. Romance is fine, but it's what takes place between the sheets that is really important to this man. So if you're a shy and sensitive Pisces who prefers moonlight walks and sweet nothings whispered in your ears, you'd better steel yourself for a very different technique. Not that he is averse to romanticism too — he isn't, and sometimes more than one would expect!

But somehow he's never been able to live down that macho image, and sometimes he doesn't want to! Although as he gets beyond his teens he realizes there's a lot more to life than sexual escapades, he unfortunately sometimes finds it hard to change his ways. They've gone on for too long now, and he may be so used to chalking up another sexual conquest that he will find it hard to settle down later in life.

Of course, not every Scorpio man is going to be a playboy all his life and that's where you come in. Once you realize that the most exciting man you've ever met, who has swept you off your feet in five seconds flat, was born under the sign of the Scorpion, you'd better go back to the 'What Are You Looking For?' and 'How Well Do You Know Yourself?' parts of the book to see if you are able cope!

But suppose you've met a Scorpio whose own particular birth chart contains certain elements that have influenced his personality almost beyond recognition, if he doesn't appear particularly sexy or his eyes aren't noticeably intense – you've got to find another way to check him out. Talk to him about his work. Scorpios are supposed to make wonderful surgeons, undertakers, butchers, scientists, psychiatrists, lawyers, reporters and spiritual healers. (You should have fun finding out if he's any of those!) It might help to know that Scorpios in general, and Scorpio men in particular, don't like giving out too much about themselves, although they do like to find out as much as possible about everyone else, and delve into that in a fairly intimate way! So if he shrugs off your casual questions with a 'No, but why don't you tell me all about you', and asks if you're married or have a live-in lover, watch out!

The Scorpio man – often the female of the species too – is fascinated by danger (*never* leave matches around a Scorpio child, playing with fire is not simply an expression with this sign). If a Scorpio man thinks he can seduce a woman who until that moment has never had eyes for anyone else, he starts to go into action fast! But remember he can cope with a quick fling very easily while maybe you cannot. For that's something else to remember with this man. He may easily have a wife and kids at home, but he certainly won't broadcast it, and it's no use looking for a wedding ring on his finger. If he's a roving Romeo his fingers will be bare!

If you've met someone new and have hazarded a guess that he seems to have some Scorpio characteristics but you're still not sure, look at the way he's dressed. Although not every Scorpio man will dress in tight jeans that don't leave much to the imagination, they will inevitably wear something that makes you take a second look. He may not necessarily be flamboyant, but he'll certainly be an expert at flaunting his sexuality, even if in an understated manner. Of course if he's got black unruly hair and flashing dark eyes, with a shirt undone to the waist showing off his manly chest, you'll know for sure you've met a Scorpion (although it's unlikely that one-twelfth of the male population will dress like that)! The majority of Scorpio males possess plenty of animal magnetism.

If you've read this far and come to the conclusion that you need some adventure in your life, you'll want to know where you're most likely to meet him! When Scorpios are interested in something it may almost become a passion — and they often have a deep range of interests. You could meet this man in a karate class (developing those sexy sinews), or a weekly group meeting where they're discussing anything from religion to the occult, but he's also a man who will turn up at a moment's notice at a party if he thinks there will be a chance of meeting someone he fancies! There really is no set hunting ground for Scorpio. He doesn't necessarily like to plan his life for weeks ahead as it's the element of the unknown that fascinates him.

If you meet him on holiday he might be snorkelling or deep-sea diving, always on the lookout for something new to do, and it's that element of danger that makes life so much more exciting for this man. Don't expect quiet romantic walks along the beach. Even though they may well take place, you must never forget that he is the sexiest man of the Zodiac, and naturally will expect you to be quite responsive too! But he's not just looking for a good-time girl who simply wants a quick fling: deep down he's searching for the ideal dream lover as much as anyone else. He's probably spent a lot of time and energy on passionate affairs with women who simply weren't right for him.

You might even score much better with him if you make him wait a while before you give in, and he may be far more interested in you if you give him the brush off at first. It may seem like gambling, but it could be worth it in the long run.

If this treatment works and the relationship with your Scorpio dream lover turns into something deeper, you'll realize he's one of the most jealous men around. Be careful! You'll have to watch him too, for even if he wants you for his wife or live-in lover, it may be hard for him to be entirely faithful, and if you become lazy and let the passion disappear from your relationship, those Scorpio eyes could start to wander all too soon.

What he needs is a woman who has a mind of her own, but is amusing, sexy and romantic too. Invincible he might be in a myriad ways, but strangely enough he's often highly vulnerable and even insecure underneath. He needs someone who will understand not only his physical needs but his inner spiritual ones too. He's highly intuitive and can read your mind like a book!

Even if he sometimes maddens you with his flirtatious ways, you'll soon realize that he's one of the most sentimental men around, so don't be upset if he insists on calling up an ex-flame to wish her a happy birthday. He can't forget things of the past even if they don't mean anything since he met you.

He loves to dine in candle-lit restaurants, where you can enjoy a few smoochy dances together after you've eaten, and he loves to be surprised with little gifts, like a pair of sexy underpants or bathing trunks, an electronic bridge or chess game, mystery or detective novels (or, if you're in the money, a fast car!). He will show as much enthusiasm as a child if he feels you've spent hours searching for something you know he'll really like.

Remember too that while he's not keen on a woman who flaunts herself in public, he won't appreciate it if you get embarrassed just because he makes it obvious he finds you alluring. He likes to see you wearing figure-flattering clothes, so make sure you keep yourself in good shape, and never, be the sort of woman who pleads a headache when you go to bed. This could wound him more than you'd think.

If anyone knows about the art of seduction it's this man, and it certainly never takes him long to get what he wants! That's why you have to keep the fire alive in your relationship with him, and never let it die! Life with a Scorpio dream lover is not going to be a bowl of cherries all the time. There could easily be moments when you feel you've landed yourself with the most feckless philanderer of all time, and then it's up to you to prove that you're the dream lover he's been searching for all his life. If you can manage that, you'll end up happier than you dreamed possible.

☆ *THE SCORPIO WOMAN* ☆

If your very own dream lover is born under the sign of Scorpio you've met the *femme fatale* of the Zodiac. She has the power to captivate the most independent men around, and even when she possesses the icy coolness of Grace Kelly, there's definitely a fire burning inside.

The sensual Scorpio woman wants to know the meaning of life from an early age. She's highly intuitive, and can read you like a book! She's inclined to take risks no other woman would take and, like the Scorpio male, she's attracted to danger. Sex to Ms Scorpio isn't something to be talked about in whispers behind closed doors, and although sex is incredibly important to her, don't start thinking you've met the nymphomaniac of all time. This woman doesn't give herself to every Tom, Dick or Harry who comes along, but to capture the heart of Scorpio, and keep it too, there has to be good sex between you or you may lose her.

A Scorpio woman will usually attract you immediately, for she stands out in a crowd. Many women born under this sign have the most wonderful eyes, often so deep you feel you could almost drown in them if she deigned to cast you a glance. She usually knows the power of her eyes, and makes them up skilfully to their very best advantage.

To capture the heart of Ms Scorpio, you have to prove you're all man — which doesn't mean flexing your muscles and moving in for the kill in the first five minutes of meeting her. Don't worry too much about how to seduce her, for if she's interested in *you* she'll make it more than clear. Seduction is easier than learning a foreign language for her.

There is no false modesty with the Scorpio woman. She makes no bones about what she thinks and feels, and isn't afraid to speak her mind, *but* she's also one of the most secretive and private ladies of the Zodiac. She could be the expert of all time when it comes to finding out about others (and in the most unobtrusive way), but woe betide you if you try to probe into the life she had before she met you. She'll clam up tight and make it more than clear that you have no business to ask.

It's not necessarily that she has a lot to hide. It is just that since she was a tiny tot she's needed her very own space where no one else could enter unless she wanted them to.

Both mentally and physically, this feeling stays with her all her life, and if you're a wise man you'll respect her wishes — and *she'll* respect you all the more in return.

If in time your Scorpio dream lover becomes your wife, just remember always to play fair. If you ever start running around with other women, that will be the end! She will think nothing of looking in your pockets to make sure there are no clues that you've been playing around. If you're worrying that you're going to land yourself with a jealous and possessive shrew, you're not. It's simply that when Ms Scorpio gives her heart and body to the man she loves, she will be one of the most loyal and loving partners around — and she expects the same from you.

Don't think that because a good sex life is essential for her she could be lacking in the romance stakes, for she's highly romantic at heart, and sensitive too. Passionate nights are one thing, but the before and after moments of making love are extremely important too.

You could almost be forgiven for thinking that this woman is someone who needs to be the stronger of the two in the partnerships she undertakes, but this isn't necessarily true. She's not as dominant as Leo, nor as aggressive as Aries, and she may have a mind of her own, but usually this woman needs a man whose inner strength can be relied upon, whose judgement she respects and who can make her laugh too. Scorpios are often so involved with the deeper side of life that they sometimes find it hard to relax and have fun. Remember, this is one of the most psychic signs around; Scorpios are fascinated by reincarnation, spiritualism, astrology and magic (sometimes both black and white), and need to get to the root of things so they can understand them better.

The Scorpio woman isn't usually difficult to spot. You've read about her eyes and can't have failed to notice her sexual allure, but while not every Scorpio is going to walk around with a plunging neckline, you can almost guarantee she'll dress in something that leaves very little to the imagination (unless at work, of course). Scorpio women are proud of their figures and will work long and hard to make sure there isn't an ounce of unwanted fat, as they like to look sexy whenever they can.

She will seem amazingly in control, and usually is! You might feel almost frightened by that simmering fire that seems to burn inside her, but if you're what she wants, you'll soon discover this sexy tigress can turn into a purring pussy cat when she's in love!

So where will you find this sensual soul mate? She may love gambling, and the excitement of winning can stimulate her even more. She won't think anything of joining a dating agency or turning up on her own at a disco, or accepting a blind date. She doesn't like routine as there has to be plenty of excitement in her life, so she hates to make plans too long in advance. She could be showing off her body at the swimming pool, health club or even at the tennis courts if she's a particularly energetic Scorpio, and she's usually not averse to going topless on the beach, knowing she looks good.

Once you've developed a good relationship with your Scorpio dream lover, you'll have fun buying her presents — black underwear, black satin sheets, musky perfumes, a water bed, the latest sexy novel, videos of her favourite movies for when you curl up in bed together, the latest model in stunning sunglasses, or some jazz tapes. She'll love figure-hugging T-shirts and her treasured brand of tight, tight jeans.

She'd probably adore a weekend trip to Paris or Amsterdam where you can go from nightspot to nightspot, but she'll equally enjoy an idyllic Greek island where she needs the minimum of clothes and can sunbathe nude, with you close by (to fend off new admirers, of course).

It's probably while walking along a deserted beach with the moon and stars shining above that you will realize there's an incredibly deep romantic yearning in your Scorpio dream lover. She needs to feel loved and desired for her soul as much as her body, so to really seduce this woman you must explore the depths of her personality, step by step, but treading warily all the time. Don't probe and pry, and remember she always *will* need that very private space.

Don't be too surprised, even if you won't admit it to yourself, if this woman is even more adept at the art of seduction than you (unless, of course, you're another Scorpio). Don't forget that she'll expect the same kind of intense devotion that she gives to you. Always remember her amazing ability to see through lies, or half-truths, and never risk the chance of seeing her Scorpio sting in action by flirting with one of her friends. She might forgive you eventually, but she'll never forget!

If you want to seduce a Scorpio . . .

DO
★ Look sexy at all times, but it doesn't always have to be in a glaringly obvious way.
★ Beg, borrow or steal (not literally) a copy of the *Kama Sutra* if you've set your heart on this dream lover.
★ Be prepared to discuss the sexual things that turn you on most (shy candidates may bow out early on).
★ Practise the smouldering eye routine yourself so you can have fun out-staring each other.
★ Keep your body in good shape – this dream lover will want to see a lot of it.
★ Just happen to have a water bed being delivered next week.
★ Keep Mr or Ms Scorpio guessing all the time – curiosity might have killed the cat but it kindles Scorpio's interest.
★ Start practising telepathy and astound your dream lover with your psychic impressions of their personality.
★ Learn to be a night person – Scorpio comes even more alive then.

DON'T
★ Ever show you could be a jealous lover.
★ Criticize Scorpio's sexual prowess, unless you want to end an affair when it's only just begun.
★ Be too intense or dramatic – this is only allowed if you're another Scorpio.
★ Fight this sign – it's the most invincible of them all.
★ Ever question Scorpio's loyalty – you'll soon learn how strong it is.

★ Get yourself involved unless you're unafraid of passion, power and possibly intrigue too.
★ Try to keep a Scorpio dream lover if deep down you realize you're not compatible sexually — it's unlikely to work.
★ Ever forget Scorpio has a need for privacy at times.

The Sagittarius Dream Lover

☆ THE SAGITTARIUS MAN ☆

Ruled by Jupiter, planet of good fortune, Sagittarians certainly often seem to have more than their share of good luck.

If you're hoping to snare a Sagittarian dream lover, always remember one vital point, that this man has to feel free! He may be the most easy-going, happy-go-lucky man you've ever come across, but if he feels there's an invisible rope around his neck he could be off before you have time to wonder what's gone wrong.

Sagittarius is the eternal optimist, one of the most positive and self-confident signs around. He has a great sense of humour, and doesn't he know it! In fact this dream lover thinks he knows *everything*, and never likes to be told he might be wrong. While he's not as headstrong as Aries, or as domineering as Leo, you can generally tell he's a Fire sign as well, for this man seems to retain his sunny personality even when the snow is inches deep or the rain is falling down from a grey and miserable sky.

If you're instantly attracted by a man who has a great sense of humour, and a boyish appeal in his smiling face, by a man who seems to accept you as a friend within minutes of meeting you, and by a man who talks enthusiastically about his hobbies and sports and is keen to introduce you to his friends, you may well have come across Mr Sagittarius (especially if you've never met anyone who can make you laugh like he can). Woody Allen, Sammy Davis Junior, Jonathan King and Billy Connolly were all born under this most outgoing of signs.

It really shouldn't be hard to guess this man's sign. This doesn't mean that he's going to stand there cracking jokes, or that he radiates humour and charm, or even that, although he's just come in from playing his favourite sport, he seems to have boundless energy still. You somehow feel instinctively that with this man you can relax and have fun, and never feel trapped by a possessive and jealous lover which, if you happen to be another freedom-loving sign, is definitely a blessing.

You feel relaxed, as if you've known him all your life. You like his boyish charm, his frank and honest way of talking, until he throws you off your stride by telling you that he doesn't like your dress, or that your eye make-up is too heavy. Yes, another good give-away with this man is that he always speaks his mind. Tactless could be the word that often describes him best, but if he ever realized that by speaking out so honestly he could wound you (deeply), he'd be horrified. He doesn't usually have an ounce of malice in him, unless it's well-deserved (and even then he finds it hard), but sometimes his humorous and witty remarks can have as much sting as you'd associated with the sign that preceeds him — Scorpio!

So if you've met someone who appears to be the life and soul of the party, is obviously optimistic, adventurous and maybe a bit of a gambler, who is perhaps moralising a little too much, and trying to tell you how to run your life when he hardly knows you, it's worth hazarding a guess and asking if he is a Sagittarius!

The symbol of Sagittarius is the Archer, and you've probably already discovered that Sagittarius is certainly adept at firing his arrows and hitting the centre of the target. If he wants everyone to stand around and listen to his latest tale of adventure, you can be sure he'll succeed. He finds it extremely easy to hold an audience, for they hang on to his every word because he makes everything sound so interesting — and once again he knows it.

But though he's a great talker he's not so good at listening to other people if he finds what they're saying boring. He may not be as restless as Gemini but he comes a pretty close second. If you want to hold his attention you'll sometimes have to work hard at it.

Sagittarians are supposed to love an outdoor life, and many of them excel at sport. If your Sagittarian dream lover is one of the exceptions to this, it must be because of his own individual birth chart, because I've rarely met a Sagittarian who prefers to curl up with a book to doing something a lot more energetic (unless there is a good sports programme on TV).

If you've found it difficult to guess the sign of the fascinating newcomer you've recently met, and feel he'll only scoff at you if you ask what month he was born, his work could be a help. Sagittarians are supposed to make good philosophers, lawyers, teachers, sports promoters, politicians, interpreters, writers and travel agents.

If he doesn't fit in any way into these, think about how he likes to dress. The Sagittarian man likes wearing casual comfortable clothes. He's not always too happy with a shirt, tie and pinstriped suit, but often has to put up with them for his job. Basically, he's probably happiest in sweatshirt and jeans. Not the most fashion-conscious of men, he doesn't care about 'designer names', if it's comfortable he'll buy it.

The Sagittarian dream lover is very special. He'll bring lots of fun into your life, and endow you with the sense of adventure that is his birthright. He loves excitement, but don't ever forget that he's a born gambler too, life *itself* being one long gamble for him. He'll take risks no other sign might take, because he knows he was born under one of the luckiest signs around. Even if he knows absolutely nothing about astrology, he probably still has an inner feeling that luck is on his side more often than not.

The trouble is that because he does feel so lucky, he sometimes makes life difficult for the people around him. He's not necessarily terribly good with money, letting his account go into the red because he's convinced something good will turn up! If you end up with a Sagittarian dream lover you may sometimes spend a few sleepless nights worrying about how you're going to pay the bills, although he'll sleep like a baby knowing things will be well. And with the Sagittarian luck, they will!

This man may not always be as romantic as you'd hope but, like the other two Fire signs, Aries and Leo, he can fall deeply in love almost at first sight, and he's certainly highly passionate. But remember that while he may swear undying love to you one moment, the next thing you know is he's arranged to go off for the weekend with his mates. However, you don't usually have to worry about him being unfaithful to you, he just hates to feel tied down. He's a free spirit and wants to stay that way.

The clever woman recognizes this need in her Sagittarian man; she allows him to feel young and fancy-free, but lets him see she's pretty independent too, and that what's sauce for the goose is equally sauce for the gander. She never becomes possessive and jealous (even if she does sometimes feel that way underneath). It's not that Sagittarius wants to keep changing partners, for if he falls head over heels in love with someone, he really does want it to be for ever.

If you're beginning to think that this man can be quite a handful, it's true, sometimes he can, but he'll be a wonderfully generous and enthusiastic lover who truly wants to make you the happiest woman in the world.

Now, having decided you like the idea of a fun-loving Sagittarian as part of your life, where are you going to meet him? Since he is such an outdoor type of man the most obvious hunting grounds will be where he's playing sport, or you could even bump into him when you're both taking your respective dogs for a walk (Sagittarians like to have animals around). He could be building up those athletic muscles in a local gym, or playing for a local football team, or you might be introduced to him when you go out with some friends to the pub or wine-bar. This man likes an active social life, and will accept an invitation at the very last moment.

Sagittarius is also the sign of 'the long distance traveller', and I've not often met Sagittarians who don't love to have the chance of setting off for somewhere new. You almost feel their bags must be permanently packed, as travel is such an integral part of their lives. If you meet your Sagittarian dream lover on holiday, you could be in for a fantastic few weeks, because somehow he becomes more romantic under the stars. But watch out, he could be looking for another Sagittarian adventure, for while he's totally honest about most things, he may hesitate to tell you there's someone else back home. Like the other two Fire signs, he's impulsive when he sees a woman he wants and with his usual Jupiter luck he'll expect you to fall into his arms without thinking about tomorrow! If all you're looking for *is* a holiday romance and you meet him this way that's fine, but you might be safer meeting Sagittarius on his own home ground than by sitting next to him on a plane to Greece.

If you are already happily involved with a Sagittarius man, but have been waiting quite a while for him to name the wedding date, you sometimes have to wait a long, long time. This dream lover is capable of feeling totally committed to a woman and keeping his freedom too. Woody Allen's relationship with Mia Farrow is just one such example: he wanted to keep his own apartment even when she became pregnant with his child. Perhaps it's just as well she's an Aquarian, for people born under that sign also value their freedom!

Sagittarius can be the most attentive lover in the world until suddenly he's off because you've started to talk about a permanent relationship. First of all you'll have to prove you're a cheerful, happy-go-lucky kind of person who doesn't have lots of bad moods because, as he's so positive himself, he can't cope with someone prone to negativity. He's a true believer that today's clouds will become tomorrow's sunshine, and while he may not like to admit he's made mistakes in his life, he's much more likely to shrug his shoulders over them, believing in his ability to overcome almost any disaster that might arise. He's a wonderful man to have around if you need moral support and encouragement. He'll lift your spirits in a moment.

The Sagittarian dream lover may call you up incessantly when you've first met, but try not to do the same to him. It's that being free bit all over again.

He loves to receive gifts, but don't overdo it − you don't want him to think you're trying to win his heart that way! It's usually easy to find presents for this man, especially if he is a sports lover − a new tennis racquet, golf clubs, or the latest line in exercise bike. Anything in the luggage line would be welcome, or a world atlas − and he loves *amusing* gifts.

So have you decided you've got what it takes to be the perfect soul mate for your Sagittarian dream lover? Do you like an action-packed life, which will certainly not be boring? Are you prepared to concede in four arguments out of five that you were wrong — just to make him feel happy? Not that he wants a 'yes woman', but he enjoys having sparring matches with you, and likes to hear you stick up for what you believe in. If you agree with him all the time he might easily get bored. As long as he's convinced he's right *almost* all of the time he's happy, and of course you have to be prepared to take his side if other people argue with him. He's one of the most loyal and supportive dream lovers around, and he expects the same loyalty and support from you.

Whilst at times he may seem like the most irresponsible man you've ever known — a true child at heart, a man who'd spend his last remaining money to celebrate an anniversary — deep down it won't take long for you to realize that a Sagittarian dream lover will keep you feeling young at heart for ever more. While your life may sometimes seem to have more than it's fair share of ups and downs, the ups will always make everything else fade away. He has this amazing ability to bring a smile to your face and to make you believe as he does that fortune really does shine on Sagittarius — as indeed it does!

☆ *THE SAGITTARIUS WOMAN* ☆

Ms Sagittarius could be your ideal lover if you've always dreamt of a woman who has a great sense of humour, is an eternal optimist, is quite prepared to be 'one of the boys' and participate in all the activities you like to indulge in. If you're prepared to put up with someone whose untidy ways would probably cause your mother to throw up her hands in horror, who manages to run out of money just when you've forgotten to bring some extra cash yourself, and if you've been searching for a woman who is independent yet prepared to give up a great deal if she falls in love with you — then search no further.

The 'independent' bit is worth thinking about a littler harder. You may think that lots of women pretend to be incredibly independent just so it doesn't look as though they're out to snare you – and that you'll soon have them where you want them once you've managed to capture their hearts. Not with your Sagittarian dream lover though, for she really *is* a free spirit. She hates to feel hemmed in, constrained, caught in a rut. She's the sort of woman who really would be prepared to end a relationship if she felt her man simply did not understand the way she thinks and feels, especially if she's got a list of things she's determined to do before she settles down.

And what Sagittarian can ever truly settle down without the chance to travel around as often as she can? You may know Sagittarians who are perfectly happy staying in the same place all their lives, but I'd like to see their horoscopes, for it's sure to be the influence of their Ascendant, the Moon and the various other planets in their own individual charts.

I'm not trying to tell you that if you capture the heart of a Sagittarian dream lover you've landed yourself with a woman who would be unfaithful the moment your back is turned. She does not need to indulge in sexual adventures, and if you're in love with each other and you satisfy her sexual needs in every way, she's unlikely to jump into bed with anyone else!

What you have to remember with the Sagittarian woman is that she hates more than anyone else to be a creature of habit, which is probably why she tends to cram her life with so many different activities that never become too much like routine. She's the kind of woman other women often envy – she always seems to radiate such a positive air. Of course there must be moments when, she too feels down and depressed, but you wouldn't often know it, and if you do see signs of despair there is bound to be a really serious reason. Things that cause the rest of us moments of heartache or depression will be thrown off like water from a duck's back with your Sagittarian woman. You're not going to see her in tears very often, but if she is unhappy, make sure that it is definitely not your fault.

The other thing about your Sagittarian dream lover is that she'll never tell you lies. The truth of the matter is she's almost too frank and honest at times. She'll tell you exactly what she thinks about every single aspect of your personality and your life, and some of it may not please you too much. It's not that she sets out to be as critical as Virgo; she doesn't even realize she *is* being critical. She simply lets you know what she's thinking. She also hates to be ordered around, even if she does fall head over heels in love with you, she's not about to be *dominated* by you!

And if in time she moves on from being your dream lover to dream partner or wife, don't expect the sort of orderly existence you may have had in the past. This woman may thrive on activity, but housework doesn't usually constitute a favourite kind. She'll do it, but in her own time. However, if you've invited the boss and his wife around for dinner, don't worry. The Sagittarian dream lover can be a wonderful hostess and the sort of gourmet cook you will be proud of. Don't forget she's travelled around, and I know many Sagittarian women who pride themselves on the international recipes they've collected on their travels.

A Sagittarian woman isn't difficult to recognize in a roomful of people. She's bound to be the one who is regaling everyone with amusing stories or chatting away about her most recent trip. She'll positively radiate vitality, self-confidence and a happy-go-lucky air. Whilst not every Sagittarian is athletically inclined, somehow you can tell this woman has amazing energy. You love the way she brings a more timid newcomer into the group, the friendly casual way she looks over at you and turns back to her listeners. You may get the impression that she's the type who likes a casual fling from time to time, but Sagittarius knows the difference between going to bed with someone on an impulse after a crazy night out, and falling in love. When she gives her heart to a man she won't want to jeopardize things by fooling around with anyone else. Her free and easy attitude won't extend to being unfaithful to the man she truly loves, so never accuse her of infidelity every time your back is turned just because she's friendly and outgoing to everyone. Remember how she hates to feel hemmed in.

If you've still found it hard to guess the sign of the woman who's captured your eye, look at her clothes. She can be dressed in the most casual way and still manage to look a million dollars.

She doesn't really care about the latest fashions or spending a huge amount on her wardrobe, and she's certainly not too proud to scout her local second-hand shop to see what bargains she can find – with her luck she usually does! She'll equally indulge in a burst of sheer extravagance and buy something that costs an absolute fortune and that she's tired of within a month, but because she *is* so independent, she won't appreciate a man who tells her off for this!

Of course you could be wondering if you can cope with this fiery, vital woman in your life, but then she will enhance it in so many different ways, that your doubts won't last for long!

If you're still looking for a Sagittarian dream lover you can find this woman anywhere the action is. She's the type to accept last-minute invitations with alacrity; to take a trip to India with a knapsack on her back; to fly to Paris or Rome for the weekend; to go jogging in the park at 7am; or to fit an exercise class into her already crowded schedule after work.

Think of Jane Fonda and Chris Evert, both perfect examples of that Sagittarian vitality, and Pamela Stephenson's zany sense of humour!

She loves life to be full of surprises, and loves receiving presents, especially if they are things to make her laugh even more. Or try a tracksuit, a dog to take for long walks (if she's an animal lover, of course) or an automatic camera.

Sagittarius is a masculine sign, like Aries and Leo, the other two Fire signs, but the Sagittarian dream lover is all woman. She's also as romantic as you could wish when the time is right. She may not take your seductive ways as seriously as you do but you have to be able to laugh together and see the funny side of life if you really want to seduce the Sagittarian woman and make her your very own.

If you want to seduce a Sagittarius . . .

DO

★ Show you can play friend as well as lover with equal ease (it's worth working at this).

★ Always show the positive side of your personality . . . it's the only one Sagittarius likes to see!

★ Let this dream lover feel inwardly free, not just at first but always!

★ Develop the ability to accept this dream lover's frank and outspoken remarks without over-reacting.

★ Make sure you're good at packing at a moment's notice — this dream lover welcomes any opportunity to travel.

★ Show that you can be just as energetic as this dream lover is — well, almost!

★ Be interested in everyone and everything that your dream lover is without intruding on his or her territory if it's obviously not appreciated!

★ Make sure that you have a great sense of humour, and make sure you like adventures too.

★ Remember life has to be fun — and that includes making love too.

★ Remember, too, that Sagittarians like to think they know all the answers. How you play that one is up to you!

DON'T

★ Ever let this dream lover see you in a really bad mood — Sagittarians hate to see the negative side of life.

★ Ever let a Sagittarian gamble too much, especially if your money is involved as well (worth remembering if you meet over a roulette wheel).

★ Ever expect a Sagittarian to be happy in a small confined space — even if it is the perfect love-nest in many other ways.

★ Expect things to happen the way *you* want them to — this dream lover hates stereotyped affairs.

★ Expect too many amorous declarations from this dream lover — Sagittarius prefers action to words.

★ Ever be too bossy.

★ Complain about the lateness of the hour if your Sagittarian dream lover suddenly decides you're the perfect partner at three in the morning after a night out on the tiles.

★ Criticize your Sagittarian dream lover for being too casual if that's the way he or she wants to play it. It's up to you to keep practicing your seductive wiles even more!

The Capricorn Dream Lover

☆ THE CAPRICORN MAN ☆

Have you been searching for a shoulder to lean on all your life? Are you tired of irresponsible men who put play before work and idle flirtations before lasting love affairs? Do you feel it's time to find a nice steady guy to settle down with, who will get on with your parents and make sure you'll want for nothing in the years to come?

Capricorn, tenth sign of the Zodiac, is ruled by Saturn, the taskmaster of the Zodiac – old Father Time or Chronos, as he was called in Greek mythology. The symbol of this sign is the Mountain Goat, and Capricorns often remind me of that animal, climbing up those difficult craggy slopes, which cause even the most sure-footed creature to stumble sometimes, until finally reaching the top. Capricorn is almost always ambitious, and will work incredibly hard to achieve his chosen position in the world, his own mountain peak.

If you're hoping to make a Capricorn dream lover your very own man, you'd best be prepared for a workaholic in the family. Of course if you're Capricorn too it could make life easier. If not, you may find it hard to accept at first!

With Saturn as his ruling planet, Capricorn almost seems to be born with old shoulders. He's wise beyond his years: at five years old his best friends are probably adults; toys are for taking to pieces to see how well they were made; other children his age are just babies to him and he doesn't have time to waste playing silly games!

But this means that your Capricorn dream lover sometimes has a harder time than most kids while growing up. However, even if the first parts of their lives do sometimes contain more pitfalls and hardships than people of other signs, from the late twenties life becomes much easier and Capricorns can live to a ripe old age happy in the knowledge that they've achieved what they set out to do.

Some pretty amazing men have been born under the sign of the Mountain Goat – Louis Pasteur, Albert Schweitzer, Mao Tse Tung, Dr Martin Luther King and Anwar Sadat, so your Capricorn dream lover is in powerful company!

As children, Capricorns tend to break arms and legs more than most other signs, suffering from weak joints and bones, especially their knees, and they sometimes have skin problems. However, they get stronger as they become older, so you don't have to worry about your dream lover in middle age. He may be more agile and athletic than you!

Do you usually have a hard time guessing someone's star sign? Let's say you've gone to a party and had a really good time, although no one has particularly taken your fancy. Then just when it's winding up, in comes another guest. Still dressed in his office clothes, perhaps clutching his briefcase, he looks as if he's still thinking about his work, not caring a hoot about being so late, and is somewhat brusque and cool in his greeting to the host. He looks as though he's the sort of man to whom relaxing and having fun is almost a sin and yes, you've guessed, you've probably come across a Capricorn.

Even if he does notice *you*, over in the corner of the room, and decides you could be worth getting to know, don't expect him to do too much about it, not yet anyway.

When introduced to him, you sense he's worrying too much about his job, money and the problems of the world. You sense he is probably as steady as a rock – but what a serious air – and he is obviously genuinely embarrassed when one of his old girlfriends plants a lipsticky kiss on his cheek. If you're thinking of getting involved with a Capricorn dream lover you'll soon learn that public displays of affection, however innocent, are definitely not for him!

You almost feel he's someone who wants to be on his own in life, at least until he's reached that mountain top! Yet there is almost something sad and wistful in his face. You sense he wants to join in and have fun with everyone else, but he's strangely unsure of himself. He's not used to large social gatherings, unless they're connected with his job.

Of course, not every Capricorn man is going to be the same and his own individual horoscope may give him a Gemini Ascendant, or a Sagittarius Moon. But it can't just be a coincidence that while writing this book I spoke to a Capricorn man who didn't have time to come to an astrology lecture I was giving. And why not? Because in addition to running *two* businesses he also had a farm which required his time and attention!

If you have met someone and are almost convinced – but not 100 hundred per cent so – start to talk to him about his work. If he *is* Capricorn it's sure to be his favourite topic. Capricorn careers are supposed to include scientists, teachers, farmers, builders, politicians, bankers, civil servants, administrators, organizers of all kinds – and tax collectors!

He'll explain to you how responsible he feels about his duties: how he can never get away until he's absolutely sure he's not left anything important undone; how he's working towards a promotion; and how he's been in the same job for quite a while because he feels people who flit from job to job are often irresponsible.

If you've decided he's the kind of man for you, but you've never held the same job for more than six months in your life, keep quiet about it, for you don't want him to sum you up as another flighty female! Don't lie, however, for Capricorns are basically honest and dislike dishonesty in others.

It's unlikely you haven't guessed his sign by now, but if he does happen to be a Goat who is the exact opposite of all this, look at how he's dressed. Even if he turns out to be a Capricorn playboy, he'll be attired soberly rather than flamboyantly. His clothes are made to last, for who has time to shop when there's work to be done? He begrudges spending too much as well. He'll look good, though. Capricorn men have lots of pride, and won't leave themselves open to criticism about the way they dress.

It may not take you very long to realize that while he's so cool, calm and self-assured on the surface, the Capricorn dream lover has a heart that beats just as fast as every other man's, and he's just as romantic too. It's simply that Saturn really is a task-master, and this planet has a firm hold on his emotions, making it hard for him to let himself relax. However, when he does decide to practise the ancient art of seduction on *you*, you can bet your life he'll be an expert. He may not have been the Casanova of all time in his younger days, but he'll have chalked up quite a few conquests by the time he's met you. Just don't ask him about them, though – this dream lover is a very private person and he won't tolerate jealousy.

The other things he won't tolerate are any criticisms about his home and family or where he lives. He's quite definitely a family man, and deep down a Capricorn dream lover is searching for the kind of soul mate who will create the perfect domestic surroundings for his future children to grow up in. Although he might hate to admit it, he cannot help being a bit of a snob, and feels it's really important to marry someone from a similar background. It probably isn't his fault. He might have had a Capricorn parent who instilled this into him from a very early age. He wants a solid marriage that is going to last, not a life of flitting from one affair to another.

So if you're not serious about your Capricorn dream lover, or think he's too practical and materialistic for you, perhaps you should search for a dream lover born under a different sign! However, of course, you know that I am generalizing in this book for your Capricorn dream lover's personal horoscope could contain a multitude of reasons why he doesn't fit the standard characterization of his sign. Don't give up too soon!

If you have decided this is definitely the kind of man you've been looking for all your life, where should you start to look for him? The best place would be at work, as he's sure to be doing overtime! Or you might find him organizing events for a local committee, or taking a few hours of leisure at a classical music concert.

If you meet a Capricorn on holiday that could be a minor miracle in itself, for how many allow themselves any time off from work? If you succeed in finding one, it's sure to be in the kind of resort where he's assured of all his material comforts without having to spend a fortune. Never forget he's an Earth sign and one of the most practical men around. If he's looking for a dream lover, it's not just for a swinging holiday affair, he's too conventional for that, and he doesn't react too well to women who start to flirt with him. He'll think they could be out to take him for a ride.

If you *can* get him to relax and let his hair down, dance the night away at a disco under the stars, have a moonlit dip in the sea, then you'll be well on the way to captivating this man's heart – but it could be on the very last night so you'll need an awful lot of patience! Still, if you do end up in bed together, he'll prove that he may be slow in making up his mind, but that he's definitely a skilful and unselfish lover.

You may have to live up to a lot with this man, but you'll soon discover the sentimental and humorous side to his personality. When you really want to please him find him a little gift that relates to a private joke the two of you have had. Little things mean an awful lot to Capricorn, but if you're buying a really special present for his birthday or Christmas, don't be wildly extravagant, find him something practical for the home or for his office – leather desk accessories, an answerphone, the latest type of calculator, a watch with a built-in alarm.

Once your dream lover has become your dream partner, make sure you don't ever let him down if he brings the boss and his wife home for a meal. Appearances are so important for this man, and when he has a wife and perhaps a family to support he becomes even more ambitious about creating the right niche for himself.

Always make sure you keep the romance alive in your relationship when the two of you are alone, for while this man is not the sort you'd expect to play around – he's spent so much of his life climbing up that ladder to success in his job – he sometimes develops a roving eye later in life if he's not completely happy at home, and that's where danger could lie. If he ever got seriously involved with someone else, much as he would hate to think of breaking up a home, he'd have the strength and determination to do just that!

Something you must always remember is that finding and keeping a Capricorn dream lover is a pretty serious business. You must live up to his ideals in a practical *and* emotional manner. He doesn't want his heart to be broken, he's concerned about the material side of life. He would hate to think you had any flighty ways, and wore low-cut dresses or extra-tight jeans. He needs to be assured you're not just looking for a good time, but that you value his company and are really keen to learn more about him.

And never, *never*, let him down on that very first date. He would take it much too much to heart, and not repeat the invitation!

Life with a Capricorn dream lover may seem to be a lot of hard work, but the efforts you put into making this man your very own dream lover will never be a waste of time.

☆ *THE CAPRICORN WOMAN* ☆

If your dream lover is a Capricorn woman, don't ever forget that with Saturn, that old taskmaster of the Zodiac, she may not seem to be one of the most light-hearted ladies around. Saturn has taught her, through experience, to control her emotions, to present such a cool and serious image to the rest of the world that they could be forgiven for feeling that she's the ice maiden personified.

A Capricorn woman has her feet firmly on the ground (yes, she's an Earth sign – could she be anything else?), but she's a woman who can attract you instantly. You sense that while she is unlikely to flaunt her femininity, let alone her sensuality, she possesses a cool and calculated charm that is all her very own, and it's definitely alluring.

True, there may be Capricorn women who are outrageous

flirts, and flit from man to man, but ten to one it will be their own individual horoscopes that create such a conflicting side to their personality. Deep down, when this woman is searching for a dream lover all her very own, she plans it to be for a lifetime, and he has to match up to her very specific ideals.

She's known from an early age that life can be tough – not that her own necessarily was, it's just that she's more realistic than some of us. She knows you have to work hard for what you want to achieve, and in her particular case Saturn often makes the first 28 or 29 years of her life the most difficult; or at least, it may not be until *after* that age that she really does know what she's trying to accomplish.

To capture the heart of a Capricorn woman it's no use expecting to sweep her off her feet by coming out with all the usual chat – the sort of compliments that could have another woman falling at your feet will cut no ice with her. She's heard it all before anyway, and she knows where it's going to lead.

No, to impress a Capricorn dream lover you have to prove that you have more than mere muscles and witty remarks, and even if you have devastatingly good looks, which will obviously have made an impression, she'll have her own stiff list of specifications you'll have to live up to before she'll consider you. Some of her bitchier friends may accuse her of being a calculating gold-digger, which would hurt her. She could never think of herself as being that way, and she's not. She just knows she needs to have security in her life, and she's prepared to work hard at achieving it for herself.

Your Capricorn dream lover may have a fairly time-consuming career herself, and don't forget that the Mountain Goat of both sexes has to climb to the top. However, if you do convince a woman born under this sign that you are the man she's been subconsciously dreaming of all her life, she will often be quite prepared to forego her own ambitions in order to run a home and help you achieve your own professional ambitions.

Whatever she does, she does well, so she usually makes a perfect wife and mother, though she's sometimes accused of being too strict! The right neighbourhood, the right house, the right school – all these things matter a great deal to Capricorn, and she'll have to get on with all your family, as indeed you'll have to with hers. You'd never have to worry about turning up at home with colleagues from work. Your place will always be spotless and there's sure to be extra food to go round.

But if you've begun to feel that you've met a sort of paragon of virtue who has little time left over for sex, don't worry. While she's not the sort of woman who'll climb into someone's bed at the drop of a hat, when she's happily ensconced in the perfect relationship she'll be as sexy and passionate as any other sign. Don't expect her to shower you with kisses or hugs in public, though. She usually finds it extremely difficult to show her emotions when anyone else is around. The sensual side of her character is for you to see, and you alone.

You may think that a Capricorn woman is easy to spot, especially if she *is* the ice maiden type, but while Princess Michael, Jill Bennet and Jane Wyman are all Capricorns, just to confuse you so are Diane Keaton and Ava Gardner!

If you're in a crowd of people and sense that someone is subconsciously sizing *you* up, and when you finally get to talk to her, she's quizzing you about what you do and where you live, before you've had the chance to ask anything about her, she might be a Capricorn. If you sense an aloofness which tends to make you feel you must come up to scratch or else she'll be off, you should be able to hazard the right guess as to her star sign.

She's bound to be dressed in a way that makes her look elegant and sophisticated no matter what her age. She has to look classy without spending a vast amount of money, and the little black dress could have been invented for her — it inevitably looks fantastic! Somehow Capricorn women seem to be blessed with the perfect bone structure and they do not need to use masses of make-up. This woman may say she hates social occasions, but when she attends one she makes absolutely sure she looks good.

She often radiates an air of self-confidence and maturity, even if she appears to be somewhat reticent about herself, and if she has a job she's bound to be striving hard to climb higher up the ladder to success. This woman doesn't do things by halfmeasures; she has the knack of getting what she wants by dint of her ambitions.

You may still feel that she is a daunting prospect, but with a

Capricorn dream lover by your side you can consider yourself very blessed. However, you'll have to convince her that it's not a sin to let her hair down from time to time, and that while Saturn may have saddled her with some of her more narrow-minded and pessimistic ways, and given her a strong sense of duty, even a Capricorn woman is entitled to feel optimistic about tomorrow too!

If you're looking for a Capricorn woman and never seem to meet one, it's not surprising. She's probably working at one thing or another, and can't afford to take time off. So keep up your search, for it's well worth while.

When you've found her, remember she likes the good things in life too, although if you shower her with extravagance she'll worry that you could be irresponsible with your cash all the time, and that would never do. Don't ever miss important anniversaries. She'll never say a word but she'll be deeply hurt inside. Search for gifts that you know she'd think were too expensive to treat herself to, even though it might be best to hide the price tag! She'd love a Gucci or Hermes scarf, portable electric typewriter, or a Filofax.

The art of seduction really does have to be an art if you want her to succumb to your charms. Never forget that underneath she is the old-fashioned type of woman, she wants lots of security, with the chance to move up in the world as the years go by. Always let her know you respect her views, and in turn you will never cease to admire her ability to keep you happy, comfortable, and in love.

Seducing a Capricorn woman may take longer than you hoped, but the end results wil make you glad you didn't give up half-way.

If you want to seduce a Capricorn . . .

DO

★ Develop a really witty sense of humour − it can melt even the coldest Capricorn's heart.

★ Always be serious about the serious things in life at the same time.

★ Accept the fact that Capricorn's career usually comes first (most of the time anyway).

★ Play the waiting game – stock up with some good books – it may take longer than you hoped.

★ Learn how to do a sexy massage that will help your Capricorn dream lover unwind at the end of a long day. . . once you've established you're the perfect partner of course!

★ Try, if possible, to have the same sort of background as your Capricorn dream lover.

★ Always remember that appearances are everything to Capricorn – who can be something of a snob.

DON'T

★ Ever embarrass this sign in public.

★ Embarrass them in private either, though that can be forgiven.

★ Expect great displays of ardent passion (unless your Capricorn's personal horoscope shows the reason why!).

★ Ever moan about the amount of time they spend working – this sign is the workaholic of all time.

★ Ever break a promise made to your Capricorn dream lover.

★ Let your image of being this sign's perfect dream lover ever slip, even if it means incredible organization!

★ Ever spend too much money when you're around this dream lover, even if it is on them. They abhor extravagance.

★ Criticize their family, their neighbourhood, their politics, or the way they make love.

The Aquarius Dream Lover

☆ THE AQUARIUS MAN ☆

Are you ready for a touch of the unexpected in your life? Can you cope with a man who can be a perfect darling one minute, but sometimes unbelievably difficult the next? Are you prepared to stand waiting and waiting while this man bumps into yet another long-lost friend? Do you realize that an Aquarian dream lover can be one of the most unpredictable, unconventional and unique men you've ever had the good fortune to meet? (Well, some women might not agree that it is necessarily good fortune, but then that's probably because they didn't learn the knack of how to get on with him!)

Aquarius, the Water Carrier, is an Air sign – not Water as so many people seem to think – and Aquarius is ruled by the inspirational planet Uranus. There is usually no way Aquarians can have humdrum lives. It's the sign of invention, of the space age, and if you think of men like Thomas Edison, Abraham Lincoln, Charles Lindbergh, Galileo, Franklin Roosevelt, not to mention Ronald Reagan, Humphrey Bogart, James Dean and Paul Newman, you'll see you've found no ordinary everyday male here!

This man will probably infuriate you a hundred times a day,

without even realizing he's doing it. He'll never behave exactly as you expect and there may be moments when you wish he had been born under any other sign but his!

If you've been introduced to one of the most interesting men you've ever met, whose intellect and friendly manner, quite apart from his striking looks, have sent a little shiver of anticipation down your spine, and if you somehow have a sneaking suspicion he's attracted to you as well, you may be in for a hard time!

When I mentioned the long-lost friend above, I should also have mentioned that this man has friends everywhere. Aquarius is very much the sign of friendship, but the trouble with many Aquarians is that they find it much easier to relate to people in general than to reveal their deepest feelings to the person they care about most.

If you've ever had an Aquarian lover in the past, your relationship may have foundered simply because you got fed up waiting for him to tell you how much he loved you. You have to realize that just because this man sometimes seems cool, aloof and detached, it doesn't mean he *is*. You might complain he spends more time thinking than feeling, but if you truly draw him out you'll discover a whole new world, and be well and truly captivated.

The Aquarian dream lover has lots of charm, there's no disputing that. He can make you believe anything he wants, but he'll always keep you guessing too. If you want a man who is never up in the clouds or sinking into downers for no apparent reason; who phones you right on the promised dot; who has a nine-to-five job he's been in for years, perhaps you should seriously consider forgetting your Aquarian.

In lots of ways, I've always felt James Dean really did epitomize the Aquarian man: he lit up the screen as an actor, and there was something unforgettable in his face, an elusiveness in his personality; with his erratic behaviour, his little boy charm, and the way he found it so hard to relate to the people close to him, is it really surprising that he became such a cult figure after his tragic death? Even today there are still many tears at his electrifying (there's a real Aquarian word) performance in *East of Eden*.

But let's assume you've just met a new man and haven't quite summed him up as far as his star sign goes. Think a little harder. Was there something just a little eccentric about him, or was it just that he was obviously bursting with original ideas that he couldn't wait to pass on to anyone who cared to listen? Did you suspect he was the kind of person who blew hot and cold in the space of a few seconds? Did you feel that he knew he was different from other men, that he didn't like a woman to make the first overture and that he wanted to remain as free as air for just as long as he liked? Was he a great flirt, and yet you felt that sex wasn't the most important thing in his life?

You could think he's Aquarius and be right about most of the above things, but when it comes to sex the Aquarian dream lover is no less sensual and passionate than any other full-blooded male. It's just that he rationalizes everything with his intellect before he gets down to the action! He needs a woman who can talk, and I don't mean about what she's done during the day, or how her girlfriend met another married man. This man is interested in Life with a capital L, he's a believer in humanity, in causes, he's a true idealist – idle gossip and chit-chat are not for him.

He's also amazingly intuitive and will be able to read you like a book. Aquarians can be in the midst of a crowd of people and instinctively know who to trust and who should be left well alone. You can bet your life this man won't give his heart away too easily, especially if it's been bruised before he developed his intuitive powers to the full.

So now you've guessed his sign, and you're dreaming about Paul Newman's electric blue eyes (yes, that's the Aquarian colour!), and wondering how to make an Aquarian dream lover recognize that you're the woman for him. Or are you still slightly confused? Do you think the way he implies he knows everything better than everyone else could mean he's really a Sagittarius, or is he being so critical about a new film that you're convinced there's a lot of Virgo in his chart?

Ask him about his job, it's not likely to be anything mundane. Aquarians are supposed to do extremely well in radio, TV, the cinema, science, politics (yes, Reagan's combined two of those!), social work, astrology, inventing, astronomy, archaeology, aviation, and anything to do with space.

Have you had a good look at his clothes? You already know this man likes to create an impact. He loves to go to a smart dinner party wearing an old pair of jeans and a sweatshirt just to shock his hostess if he thinks she's a bit of a snob; or there'll be an ethnic look about his shirt. He likes to feel comfortable, but he has an eye for fashion that is all his very own, and he's usually ahead of his time.

You've also quickly realized that while he's following every conversation with what may appear to be rapt attention, he's sometimes off in a world of his own — although he won't miss a word. It's just that his attention span can't cope with someone who goes on and on over the same old subject, not when he has something of vital importance to impart himself — his ideas on nuclear energy, or what's happening in Nicaragua, or the latest left-wing cause.

You're beginning to understand that this man needs excitement in his life, and that he's definitely a very special kind of man. So if you're currently on your own and have decided you're going to search for an Aquarian dream lover, where do you think he's likely to be? To give you a clue, you'll often find that clubs and societies attract them — anywhere they have the chance to express their inventive and original ideas to as many people as possible. They invariably like to study unusual subjects, and you could come across this man at an evening class for photography or astrology, or on a march or anti-nuclear rally — his humanitarian ideals never falter.

If you meet an Aquarian on holiday you're in for an exciting time, but you won't find him in your everyday run-of-the-mill place. No, he's probably planned a vacation totally different from all his friends. He may be travelling on his own (he knows it won't stay that way for long), and if you strike up an acquaintanceship with him don't expect it to turn into an immediate holiday romance, even though you might hope it does! You may have to put up with being just good friends for a while, unless his own particular horoscope gives him a more passionate personality! You'll have to make yourself so irresistible and unique in every possible way that he won't be able to ignore you. Why not practise being as cool and aloof as him?

If you're reading this because you've fallen head over heels in love with an Aquarian man and are prepared to put up with his unpredictable ways, never get too possessive. Just because he's out late it doesn't mean he's in bed with someone else. He's a loyal man when someone has captured his heart . . . just think how long Paul Newman has been married to Joanne Woodward, or Ronald to Nancy.

The Aquarian dream lover is definitely not a man who likes to feel tied down. Life has to be something of an adventure for him, and he likes to do things on the spur of the moment. It's hard for him to be punctual because of this.

He needs a woman who likes to have a life of her own, as well as being with him, but even a freedom-loving Aquarian has a jealous streak. Because deep down he's completely honest he won't appreciate it if you tell him any lies. If you're clever you'd never even try, for he will be very adept at reading your mind. Don't think that just because he is often so cool and detached it means he's not summing everything up. He can be as psychic as Scorpio, and just as invincible too.

Because he may be bad at remembering your birthday or sending you a card on Valentine's Day, you might feel you're entitled to give him the same behaviour in return, but he's amazingly sentimental underneath. Although he'd never show he was hurt, he'd hate to think you'd forgotten any of *his* important dates!

It's no use thinking that if you've managed to convince your Aquarian dream lover that you're the perfect soul mate he'll start to live a more conventional and less unpredictable life. That would be too much like expecting a leopard to change his spots.

If the mental stimulation between you never dies, your sex life will always be good, but the two have to go hand in hand. He can be as passionate about his various causes as he is about you. It's not that you'll have to take second place, but you'll have to be prepared to discuss his ideals long into the night too.

Life with this man can be a lot of fun, and you'll never be bored; you may be infuriated at times, but you'll be deliriously happy too. He's a wonderful man to surprise with presents. He likes gadgets of every kind, and the latest space technology is often one of his hobbies – buy him a telescope! Some software for his computer, an automatic slide projector, a solar energy calculator or an aluminium briefcase could please too.

Although it may have taken a long, long time for him to reveal his deepest emotions to you, once you've broken the barrier he'll be a perfect lover, and the best friend you ever had in your life.

☆ *THE AQUARIUS WOMAN* ☆

If your dream lover is born under the sign of Aquarius, she'll have many of the same characteristics as her male counterpart for, of course, Uranus is her ruler too.

Never forget, however, that a woman's emotions *do* differ from a man's.

An Aquarian woman may appear to be cool, aloof and in her own little world, but she's as passionate as any of the fiery sun signs when she decides to let her hair down. It's just that she's searching for a man whose intellect can match her own, and whom she feels is the perfect mate in bed and out. She doesn't care about your money, she'll be more interested in knowing you have a good brain. She's not the kind of woman who'll rush head-long into an affair, as you have to become her friend before you become her lover – and that won't happen overnight. It will probably take you a while to realize she's even interested in you anyway!

The Aquarius woman is often deeply involved in one cause or another: Vanessa Redgrave has her politics, Mia Farrow has adopted many children (as well as having many of her own); Farrah Fawcett determined to play a battered wife in a real-life movie story to try and help people understand the problem. Listen to some of Carole King's lyrics. Zsa Zsa Gabor is also Aquarius, and her cause often seems to be making sure her real age is never revealed and beating the record for the largest number of husbands!

If you fall so heavily for an Aquarian dream lover that you end up marrying her, don't expect a humdrum life: the house may be full of people just when you want to relax, and you may have to wait for dinner because she's writing up the minutes of her local charity committee's last meeting. Don't try to cheat on her. She'll read it in your eyes, and while she's a great advocate of freedom for both sexes, it doesn't usually include hopping into someone else's bed. That's the way she conducts her life and it's the way you'll need to conduct yours if you want to keep her by your side.

This woman knows what independence is all about — it's one of her greatest assets — and she's prepared to use it time and time again if need be. She may be one of the most unpredictable, unconventional, maddening and elusive people you've ever met (though if you also happen to be an Aquarian, you'll have the same traits yourself!), but she's sure to be one of the most fascinating too. Of course you'll never quite know what to expect from one day to the next. It's not that she changes moods as often as Gemini, it's just that when you expect her to behave in one particular way, that's when your best laid plans go awry.

She knows she's different from other women, and she revels in it — why not? She excels at social events. This woman is bound to have more acquaintances than anyone you know; close friends may be counted on the fingers of one hand. She'll do anything for anyone, is a sucker for lame dogs, but she doesn't usually want to get too close to more than a few very special people, and sometimes even they find it difficult to believe that she cares for them as deeply as she does.

If ever there was an expert at hiding her deepest feelings it's Aquarius. It's almost as if someone born under this sign feels that to reveal the emotions shows a weakness, something that could be used against them, perhaps taking away their freedom, or leaving them too vulnerable in the future.

Yet this woman has a unique strength which gives her the ability to get what or who she wants! She's the woman of the future — her ideas are often way ahead of her time, and she's an expert at expressing them to anyone who cares to listen.

It may seem a time-worn cliche, but what this woman is really looking for is someone who understands her and until you break through the surface of her exterior personality — which can sometimes be a long hard struggle — you won't really know what makes Ms Aquarius tick! She's not looking for a 'yes man', nor is she looking for someone who's only interested in bossing her about (although her opposite sign of Leo could make a perfect partner for her as long as she manages to respect his mind as well as his domineering manner).

The Aquarius woman's unconventional approach to life can sometimes be hard to take, but when it comes to sex she can be as down to earth as the rest of us. However, if you assume she's yours for ever simply because she's started an affair with you, *you* could be wrong, because sex alone isn't enough for her — there has to be a true blending of the minds as well.

It won't take you long to realize you have come across one of the most complicated of women. She's a romantic idealist who can be warm and loving one minute, detached and aloof the next. She may like to do her own thing, but at least she won't ever be dishonest — so you'd better be the same!

If you've just met a woman like this you must have guessed her sign by now. If not, draw her out in conversation a little more, then look at how she's dressed. She loves ethnic clothes, and putting together a bit of this and a bit of that — something she found in a jumble sale could be belted with an Italian designer belt. She loves to stand out in a crowd with the most original way of dressing she can find, and find it she will, without having to spend a fortune either.

Perhaps she'll have a job that is infinitely more interesting than most of the other women you've met recently — it certainly won't be nine to five. If you've always dreamed of finding an Aquarian woman to be your soul mate, where should you look? She could be vigorously involved in local politics; doing part-time social work as well as having another job; or looking after under-privileged children. She's a motivator, she likes to get things done and nothing is too much trouble when she truly believes in it. As one of the most friendly, outgoing and sociable signs around though, she will also be where there is plenty going on. She's the sort of person who loves last-minute party invitations, or who would think it a joke to put an ad in the personal columns.

Her likes and dislikes are various, and are as unusual as she is. She likes to be surprised *and* hates to be forgotten. One day she'll enjoy being fussed over, the next day it could drive her mad!

177

She'll go anywhere, do anything — and she wants to be unique in every way. She may pretend she's not looking for someone to tame her wild spirit, but there's one part of her that would welcome the man who could, provided he's someone she could always look up to and who wouldn't try to dominate her 24 hours a day.

Present giving can be a real pleasure with this woman — she is often a child at heart when it comes to unpacking parcels. The more original the gift the happier she'll be, so make sure you give yourself more than just an hour to look for a crazy T-shirt or a way-out piece of stainless steel or silver jewellery. She'd also like lots of tropical plants for her home, a cordless hairdryer, hi-tech luggage, an alarm clock with radio and phone, and a tempura set.

Seducing an Aquarian woman is definitely an art, and you have to have patience. Even Casanova would have to try and try again before Ms Aquarius would fall for his charms as she's no overnight conquest. But she's well worth waiting for, so don't give up too soon!

If you want to seduce an Aquarius . . .

DO

★ Play being as cool, detached and unemotional as this dream lover sets out to be.

★ Make sure you always have plenty of interesting things to talk about.

★ Remember this sign is devoted to causes of all kinds, especially minority causes, so make sure you have a few favourites of your own.

★ Work on ways to seduce this dream lover's mind first. . .

★ Make sure this dream lover feels you'll always be a good friend even if you're not sexually compatible.

★ Remember they like surprises — which should give you scope for a few interesting and unusual ideas!

★ Always understand this dream lover is a free spirit and your seductive techniques must be very carefully and subtly planned.

★ Always praise this dream lover's aspirations — and help them achieve them when you can.

DON'T

★ Ever try to pin Aquarius down to times or places.

★ Ever try to indulge this dream lover in long conversations on the phone.

★ Make a scene if this dream lover turns up in their oldest clothes when you're supposed to go off to a cocktail party — Aquarius thrives on being different.

★ Use your seductive wiles when Aquarius clearly isn't in the mood.

★ Be upset if this dream lover is suddenly coldly sarcastic — it's not just Cancerians who have moods you know!

★ Even bother to fall for this dream lover if you want fiery passion every night.

★ Imply you want to get involved too early on — in fact don't ever imply you want to get *too* involved!

★ Ever be the clinging type — Aquarius has to feel free.

The Pisces Dream Lover

☆ THE PISCES MAN ☆

Do you sometimes wonder if there is any romance left in the world, why all we hear about is sex, violence and political unrest? Do you dream of a man who is warm, compassionate and sensitive, and who — gazing soulfully into your eyes — will softly whisper all those words you're longing to hear?

I would be accused of being unrealistic if I stated outright that Pisces was the most romantic sign of the entire Zodiac, and anyone could retort that a Cancer or Libra would be equally romantic. We're all individuals, and every horoscope is unique, based on the date, time and place of a person's birth, but since a book can only generalize, I still have to stick my neck out and say that if you want *true* romance in the age-old sense, go for the sign of the Fish!

Pisces is ruled by Neptune, the planet of inspiration, and Pisceans are amongst the most creative people around (although not necessarily the most practical). You have to remember that the symbol of Pisces, last of the Water signs, is two fish swimming in opposite directions. Pisces has to make that choice, upstream to success, or perhaps an easier swim downstream that could lead to nowhere. Time and time again astrologers talk about Pisceans looking at the world through rose-coloured spectacles, building dream castles in the air, avoiding reality, evading the main issue ...

If you've met a man who has the most beautiful eyes you've ever seen, which seem almost to be twin mirrors of his soul; if you sense that he is probably one of the most gentle and tender lovers you could ever meet; if there's a little boy lost look about him, a sweet vulnerable charm that makes you want to take him under your wing, you're probably falling under the spell of a Piscean!

Music, art, dancing, photography, all have more than their share of Pisceans – think of Caruso, Chopin, Rimsky-Korsakov, Michelangelo, Renoir, the Earl of Snowdon, Nijinsky and Nureyev.

Pisceans always express their romantic feelings in a very special way, and your Pisces man is sure to be a veritable spinner of dreams. He's also one of the most intuitive men you've met, and he'll soon be reading your thoughts, so beware!

If you become involved with a Pisces dream lover there could be an almost telepathic communication between you. I've noticed many times with my Piscean friends – of both sexes – that they always seem to sense when I have something special to tell them; even if we haven't spoken for a while, the phone will ring just at the moment I've thought I must call them.

It's not difficult to guess this dream lover's sign even if his eyes haven't given you a clue. He may be very shy when you first meet, and if it's at a party he'll probably let everyone else chatter away while he's silently summing you up. Don't forget he's probably searching for a dream lover too, and his trouble is that he's so idealistic and impressionable that he can sometimes fool himself in his search.

The sad thing about Pisces is that if his illusions have been shattered, if he's suffered too many broken love affairs, he starts to become depressed and negative, trying to find ways to drown his sorrows. That's where trouble can start, for Pisces is one sign that can be drawn to alcohol or even drugs too easily. I am generalizing once again so don't get the idea that every Piscean is an alcoholic or drug addict! He's sure to have had some unhappy romances in his life, though, for when Pisces truly gives his heart he wants it to be for keeps and he puts his lover on such a high pedestal she sometimes cannot live up to his ideals.

So perhaps you should examine your motives for wanting to meet this man before you go any further. If you're just looking for a good time, please try not to shatter this dream lover's ideals about love and romance. Unless his own particular chart shows otherwise, the Pisces dream lover is looking for more than that. He needs a woman who is prepared to enjoy looking through his rose-coloured spectacles from time to time, and help him to spin his dreams.

If you've just been introduced to someone new, and want to check out your sneaking feeling that he could be the sign of the Fish, ask him about his work. The careers usually listed for Pisces are writer, actor, poet, dancer, musician, clairvoyant, nurse, teacher, social worker, sailor, priest and photographer. Lots of Pisceans have different careers, of course, but the one probable constant is that whatever they're doing is not necessarily for the money, but because they *really like* the work. The Pisces dream lover, in fact, is not your materialistic sort of money maker, and there's worse to come. This man is usually *terrible* with money – no matter what he earns he finds it hard to keep. It's not always that he's very extravagant, but he's definitely the sort of man to send you a dozen red roses when he's overdrawn at the bank! Somehow money and a Pisces are always soon parted. He's a soft touch for anyone who comes along with a hard luck story, and hopeless at balancing his accounts. He always seems to spend more than he earns, and if he doesn't have a good accountant he's usually in trouble when it's time to fill in those tax returns.

You're beginning to get a picture of Pisces, but if you're still not quite sure you've guessed correctly, take a sideways look at how he's dressed. He may not be the best dresser you've ever met, but there is sure to be a blending of colours and fabrics that show his artistic taste and sense of colour. He hates anything too loud and garish and he's embarrassed by women who overdress too. If those soulful eyes haven't got you, his choice of after-shave or cologne is sure to put you in the mood for romance!

It won't take you long to realize that you've met a man who can make many of your own dreams come true. He is someone who will never change partners again if he has his ideal soul mate by his side. But while his intuition and wisdom should never be under-rated, this man is often a mystery even to himself. He's an actor on a vast stage. He has to help everyone who has problems of any kind but often he's the worst at helping himself. He can sink into a sloth of apathy or rise to the heights of happiness; his sense of humour is phenomenal but he's not ashamed to let you see his tears.

Maybe you haven't come across this romantic dreamer yet, so where should you begin to search? Pisceans often love yoga, meditation classes or dancing. They love the theatre (if ever there was a born actor it's Pisces), art galleries, music, helping on a charity committee, sailing and fishing (don't forget he's a Water sign!), or rescuing a stray dog.

If you're lucky enough (yes, some women do consider it luck!) to meet a Pisces on holiday, you can rest assured it will be one of the most romantic involvements you've ever known. You see, no matter how he behaves outwardly, deep down he's looking for a true soul mate. This is the man with whom to take those moon-light walks along the beach; to dance the night away under a starlit sky; to gaze at sunrises and sunsets whispering sweet nothings into each others' ears. He's not looking for a one-night stand, he's looking for commitment right from the start, but the trouble is that he often fools himself. He wants to fall in love so much it can happen too fast, and he will be building those castles in the air before you've really got to know each other that well.

If you've ever been involved with a Pisces man you'll have to acknowledge the bliss of being treated like the only woman in the world – to be paid compliments that you know he means (and it's not just that he's trying to get you into bed). If it's real old-fashioned romance you're searching for, with a tender, caring lover whose only wish is to make you feel wonderful, this is the perfect man to meet both on holiday and at home too. And if you fall for him the way he falls for you, the two of you will probably forget about everyone else around and only have eyes for each other from now on.

The major snag is reality. He can escape from it while he's on holiday, but he's fooling you as well as himself if he pretends it doesn't exist. It's not that he wants to deceive you, but you'd better make sure he isn't already spoken for — albeit unhappily, perhaps. He can actually pull the wool over your eyes much too easily, simply because he's so high up in the clouds with his dreams of happiness ever after.

Never accuse him of something unjustly — remember this is a highly sensitive soul, for he'll be deeply wounded by a hurtful remark or action.

He's also one of the most sentimental men around — yes, even more than Cancer! He'll delight in occasions such as St Valentine's Day when it's the perfect opportunity to shower you with little gestures of his love and take you to a favourite candle-lit bistro. He loves to receive little gifts that you've obviously chosen with a great deal of thought: a dozen pairs of expensive French or Italian socks or a soft cashmere sweater in his favourite colour; the aftershave he loves but can't afford; new swimming trunks; records of his favourite singers; or some silver champagne goblets.

He may be shy to start with, but he's a warm cuddly lover once he's found his ideal woman. He doesn't like anyone too forceful, and it may take him a while to pluck up the courage to ask you for that very first date. Don't push it with Pisces. If it's meant to be, it will happen. He knows that well enough and so must you!

Of course your life with a Pisces dream lover won't always be smooth sailing, but what relationship is easy *all* the time? The very fact you know he's bad with money and sometimes hopelessly impractical should help you know just how to cope. (Although if you're another Pisces, perhaps you should employ a really good accountant to sort you both out. It will save an awful lot of trouble in the long run.)

If you're not too disillusioned to believe that there is still a man out there who has the same ideals and aspirations as you, and who will do all in his power to make *your* dreams come true, then you should forget about the other eleven signs of the Zodiac. Concentrate on making your Pisces dream lover realize that he doesn't have to search any more, for you're the one woman who can fulfil all his needs, giving him the tender loving care he craves so much.

☆ *THE PISCES WOMAN* ☆

It shouldn't take you long to ascertain if your dream lover was born under the sign of Pisces — and that's *without* asking her if she was born between February 19 and March 20! Without any doubt Pisces is considered the most romantic and dreamy-eyed sign in the entire Zodiac, and romance is what makes the world go round for the Pisces woman.

Somehow there always seems to be something very special about the eyes of a Pisces woman. You feel yourself melting away as she softly gazes your way. You sense the warmth, sincerity and understanding that she generates and you are convinced that at last you've met a woman who will be a true soul mate, taking care of your needs, soothing away your problems, and loving you for ever more.

As a child, the Pisces woman probably spent hours reading fairy-tales about enchanted cottages and fairy godmothers, and as she grew older she may have been enraptured by the tales of Camelot — seeing herself as Guinevere, of course! The Pisces woman is always searching for true romance, and no matter how often her hopes may be dashed by one disaster or another, she never gives up! Just think of two of the women born under this sign — Elizabeth Taylor (those wonderful violet eyes!) and Liza Minelli.

Of course, committed feminists are sure to scoff at Ms Pisces. They'll feel she's letting the side down, using her feminine wiles to capture a mere man, but what do you care what other women think about her? For having met this adorable dream lover, you're not about to let her drift away.

To capture the heart of a Pisces woman you'll have to be pretty romantic yourself. It's no use being a hard-bitten, cool calculating and materialistic man if you want to have this woman by your side. But perhaps you ought to be fairly practical — at least where money is concerned — for the women of this sign are not noted for their ability to handle their finances. (If your particular Pisces gets up in arms about that and has proved that I'm wrong, it's probably because she's got lots of Taurus, Virgo or Capricorn in her own individual chart, for I can only generalize in this book.)

Of course if your Pisces dream lover ends up as your live-in partner or wife, you will probably have a few fights about why the housekeeping money is gone by Tuesday night, or why she forgot to collect your best suit from the cleaners. The list of things she's likely to forget is probably endless, but then she has so many other assets that make your life such bliss!

Always remember that sweet words and loving gestures tend to be much more important to her than a heavy physical affair. It's not that sex isn't important, simply that sex alone is not a priority for the Pisces woman. If you're about to blaze in with your full seductive wiles, it's also worth remembering that you need romantic surroundings, otherwise you're starting off at a disadvantage!

If you think that seducing this woman could be a piece of cake, watch out! She's probably been disillusioned once or twice in her life through building those castles in the air, and she could be a lot wiser now. Too many men have taken her sweetness and innocence for granted, played around with other women, knowing full well she'll be waiting with stars in her eyes when they finally return. If this has happened to your Pisces dream lover, she's not going to let it happen again. However, she'll need someone who has a great deal of inner strength and who can brighten up her days when she feels depressed, who will never hurt her feelings but somehow manage to push her into organizing herself a little better.

The Pisces woman hates arguments, hates to be teased, and above all abhors any form of cruelty to people or animals, but for all her soft and sensitive exterior, this woman can be devious too! (According to one lovely Piscean actress I know well, and who was born in February, it's only Piscean women who were born in March who possess this particular trait!) Ruled by Neptune, the Pisces woman is probably immensely creative and artistic, but is shy about letting anyone see her talents. She needs lots of encouragement and support to push her into the limelight.

If you've met someone who almost seems to fit the description of Pisces, but you're not completely sure, look at how she's dressed the next time you meet. It's sure to be ultra-feminine, with flowing skirts and flowery prints in summer, never anything too severe. She likes to look pretty, for this woman has a flair with fabrics and colours. Her eye for beauty enables her to pick the perfect fashions for her own particular personality, to enhance that aura of romance surrounding her.

If you've never come across a Pisces woman and feel she sounds the perfect mate for you, where should you start to search? Remember that she is often shyer than most of the other signs, but with her interest in the arts she's sure to go to lots of concerts and art galleries, and if she has conquered her shyness she might belong to an amateur dramatic group (for Pisceans of both sexes are definitely born actors at heart, whether they admit it or not). She might be at the local swimming pool or sitting watching the tide go out. (Don't forget Pisces is a Water sign, its symbol being two fish swimming in opposite directions).

Even if she does present a strongly independent personality when you meet her, once you've talked to her for just a while you'll sense that little girl lost appeal that has always made her such a perfect dream lover. She can be changeable in her likes and dislikes though.

The art of seduction must be finely tuned really to capture her heart, and because she's such a sentimental soul don't ever dare to forget her birthday, Valentine's day, the anniversary of the first time you met, her dog or cat's birthday, her favourite flowers. Things that may not always be of paramount importance to other signs shine out like beacons in this woman's mind.

She loves to be taken to intimate little romantic restaurants, where her favourite music plays softly in the background, and where there are candles on the tables instead of bright neon lights above. For holidays she loves to be near the water (as if you hadn't already guessed that), and when you're buying her a present, search for the prettiest lingerie you can find (but nothing too blatantly sexy), or some pretty patterned tights; books of her favourite poetry; her favourite scent in bath and body lotions; a soft angora sweater to match the colour of her eyes. It won't take you long to realize just how much she appreciates the slightest little sentimental gift, and don't forget to send her flowers on every possible occasion.

The Pisces woman may sometimes be infuriatingly indecisive, even lazy, and she'll off in her own private reveries just when you feel like talking about the upswing in gold prices! But she's a real woman, and if you're prepared to share her dream you'll discover a myriad memorable moments to make life a lot more pleasurable, with a wealth of romantic bliss to keep you happy and contented ever more.

If you want to seduce a Pisces. . .

DO

★ Think up ways to prove that old-fashioned romance still exists.

★ Let your romantic messages show in the way you look into this dream lover's eyes − it should have the desired effect.

★ Give the impression of being incredibly tender and compassionate, even on days when you're in a foul mood!

★ Show that you'd be a wonderful shoulder to lean on.

★ Show that you love listening to romantic ballads.

★ Show that you are never ashamed to cry in sad movies.

★ Show that children and animals are important to you.

★ Let your touch be soft and caressing when you get close to this dream lover.

★ Make it seem you've never been in love before and this is really *it*!

DON'T

★ Ever hurt this dream lover's feelings in any way at all.

★ Go on about their impractical ways with money − they already know they're impractical.

★ Give the impression that love is just a game to you.

★ Imply you're *not* interest in old-fashioned romance but that it's action you want. You could end up getting neither.

★ Have eyes for anyone else when you're with this dream lover.

★ Be nasty to anyone, including your neighbour's cat.

★ Ever moan if you're woken up with a declaration of love in the middle of the night.

★ Ever forget that Pisces truly is looking for a dream lover, not just a sexual playmate.

Staying on Cloud Nine

You've finally arrived at that magical moment when you've found your dream lover, with both of you utterly convinced that the chemistry is right and that nothing will ever tear you apart. Perhaps it's champagne time. You may have set the date for a wedding, or simply started living together.

You've mastered all the tricks in the seductive art of astrology and you're determined to remember them for ever, giving yourself a quick refresher course if it should ever be necessary. Now it won't matter if you read that a fiery Aries personality can scorch your Taurean heart, or that Leos really *do* hate taking second place even to another Leo, for the seductive wiles of your own star sign can win hands down!

You've mastered the techniques of astrological seduction, and learned to become more tolerant, more understanding and, of course, more irresistible. If you're a Piscean, you've even learned to become more practical too! If you happen to be a Gemini who *still* wants to flirt with other people even when you have captured your ideal dream lover, you'll make sure you're very, very discreet. And if you're a Cancerian who has convinced your new-found partner that the best place to be is at home with you, you'll make sure you try harder to be loveable when it's full Moon time. Now you've brought the game of love to its best possible conclusion, you have to make sure you keep it that way! If you've really digested all the information in this book, you will have realized that the more we learn about our own star-sign personalities, and our dream lover's too, the easier it is to be compatible. And now you know that even if you *are* opposite signs of the Zodiac you can still get on wonderfully well with each other.

With the aid of your own intuition, common sense, and a memory bank full of your astrological seductive techniques, you now know just how to keep your dream lover by your side. Even if this ideal partner is a passionate Scorpio, you've realized that good sex isn't enough, that it isn't only Gemini who requires plenty of mental stimulation, and that romantic Pisces can be perfectly willing to learn how to be a little more practical too. You also know by now that astrologically there are positive and negative characteristics in all of us – and you've learnt how to conceal any negative ones that could be lurking in the background.

So keep it all up. Have fun understanding your dream lover's personality even better, make the romance stay alive in your relationship, and remember how it was when you first realized you were meant for each other!

Use the seductive art of astrology all the time, ensuring your relationship grows even stronger. For once you've truly mastered this art, whatever sign your dream lover is born under, you will be an expert at knowing just how to keep him or her as your dream partner for many years to come.